More Praise for *The Power of Commitment*

"We all start out in love and committed, vowing to love till death us do part. Tragically, less than half of us succeed. What we need to keep things going is a book like this that lays out step-by-step what commitment looks like and, more important, how it behaves. It's amazing that a book so vital and important can also be so much fun, so easy to read, easy to understand, and enjoyable. If you're in love and committed and want to stay that way, competently and joyously, buy this book!"

—**DIANE SOLLEE**, founder and director, www.smartmarriages.com

"Scott Stanley brings his groundbreaking research to the heart of this very important book. A must-read for individuals and couples who wish to revitalize and solidify their marriage. This is one of the finest books on divorce prevention ever written. Dr. Stanley helps individuals and couples revitalize their marriage and insure it for safekeeping. Scott Stanley explains why couples can grow apart while living an ordinary, seemingly productive life. He also provides a practical, research-based approach for avoiding the pitfalls. This book carries the reader with its authenticity and, sometimes sobering, ring of truth. A must-read for those who want a happy marriage."

—**PAT LOVE**, author, *The Truth About Love*

"In my position here at The Center for Marriage & Family Studies I'm often asked what I think are the very best, the most practical and helpful relationship resources. For years at seminars and workshops across the country I recommended *The Heart of Commitment* and now I'm delighted to recommend Dr. Stanley's most recent and even more practical book, *The Power of Commitment*. The material in Chapters One and Two alone is worth the price of the book. Without genuine commitment, what many people call love is little more than a superficial caricature of the real thing. Once again, Scott goes beyond merely suggesting new skills and exercises to helping the reader actually redefine what a healthy marriage can be. If you have a good marriage, this book will help you go to the next level. If you're discouraged and thinking of giving up, reading this book will restore your hope and renew your heart."

—**GARY J. OLIVER**, executive director, The Center for Marriage & Family Studies; professor of psychology and practical theology, John Brown University; and coauthor, *Raising Sons and Loving It!*

"In *The Power of Commitment*, marriage researcher Scott Stanley cuts through the cultural misinformation (much of it coming from therapists) that threatens and undercuts marriage in our society. Stanley is grounded in his religious commitment, his mature practicality, and in the research and literature on marriage and divorce. This is a basic and practical book brimming with wisdom and hope."

—**FRANK PITTMAN**, author, *Grow Up! How Taking Responsibility Can Make You a Happy Adult*

THE
POWER
OF
COMMITMENT

A Guide to Active, Lifelong Love

SCOTT M. STANLEY

Foreword by Gary Smalley

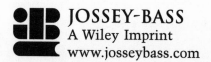

JOSSEY-BASS
A Wiley Imprint
www.josseybass.com

Published by Jossey-Bass
A Wiley Imprint
989 Market Street, San Francisco, CA 94103-1741   www.josseybass.com

Jossey-Bass books and products are available through most bookstores. To contact
Jossey-Bass directly, call our Customer Care Department within the U.S. at 800-956-7739,
outside the U.S. at 317-572-3986, or fax 317-572-4002.

Jossey-Bass also publishes its books in a variety of electronic formats. Some content that
appears in print may not be available in electronic books.

Scripture quotations are from The Holy Bible, English Standard Version, copyright
©2001 by Crossway Bibles, a division of Good News Publishers. Used by permission.
All rights reserved.

Book design by Suzanne Albertson

Library of Congress Cataloging-in-Publication Data
Stanley, Scott, date.
The power of commitment : a guide to active, lifelong love / Scott M. Stanley ; foreword
by Gary Smalley.—1st ed.
       p. cm.
Includes bibliographical references.
     ISBN 0-7879-7928-7 (alk. paper)
  1. Love. 2. Marriage—Religious aspects—Christianity. 3. Commitment. I. Title.
     BF575.L8S755 2005
     306.872—dc22

                                                    2004026723

Printed in the United States of America
FIRST EDITION
PB Printing 10 9 8 7 6 5 4 3 2 1

• CONTENTS •

I first met Scott Stanley in 1994, and I've come to know him well. Since we met, I've become convinced that he is onto deep truths about commitment in marriage. If you've ever searched for them, you were probably surprised to find so few books focusing on this subject, especially when we know that commitment is the foundation of success in marriage. Why is it that married couples separate? What helps them stay together in a loving way? Why do some couples thrive, while others barely make it from one day to the next? *The Power of Commitment* brings together so much of what I've wanted to see in the hands of couples. I believe that this book will not only help you stay together, but, more important, it will inspire you to enter into the fullest kind of life possible in marriage. The book you are holding in your hands has become one of my favorite marriage books. The principles, the stories, and the research-based strategies will make a difference in your marriage if you act on their powerful truths.

It is reassuring to me that the insights presented in this book are based on sound marital research. I am awed by the way Scott Stanley takes research and makes it come alive, finding new depth and insights about a topic that too many have come to think of as boring. Make no mistake—there is nothing boring about this book. It's about the thoughts and actions that give life to a marriage. It is about living passionately yet realistically in the fullness of a life together. You, dear reader, are in for a real treat, for here you will find encouragement and solid instruction founded on timeless principles. Stanley offers you practical insights beyond what you ever thought could come of the topic of commitment. You will be helped to visualize a richer, deeper path for your own marriage.

Many in our society have come to believe that commitment is merely fulfilling an obligation: staying through thick and thin when you'd rather leave. There are indeed times in most marriages when commitment is hard and even painful. But, as Stanley shows you here, commitment that merely propels us forward is not the only kind of commitment that matters. That kind is important, but there is another side of commitment, and all that comes with it, that compels us to give and invest in our marriages in ways that lead to greater joy, togetherness, and confidence. This book is about that life-giving, thriving kind of commitment. The great news is that there are many practical suggestions that you can act on to keep your marriage strong and happy, and this book is full of them.

Commitment is not about making a choice once and for all, on one day at the start of a marriage; it is about making many right choices every day and every week and every month. For example, there are many opportunities you will have in a life together where you can choose to give to your mate with the kind of love that propels a marriage beyond mere stability to dynamic vitality. The pages to follow can cultivate within you habits of giving that promote and protect your love. The ideas in *The Power of Commitment* will grab you and shake you up so that you'll no longer settle for ho-hum commitment.

Some have said that marriage is an outmoded idea and that lifelong love is really not possible. Nonsense. Your heart desires something that is truly possible if only you and your mate (or mate-to-be) apply yourselves. It takes effort and wisdom to build a deeply satisfying marriage. If you supply the effort, this book will give you a large dose of the wisdom you need.

I hope and pray that you will experience the fullest measure of what life can be in marriage. Now it is your turn to see why I have been so excited about Stanley's work and the ideas he presents here.

Gary Smalley
Branson, Missouri

• ACKNOWLEDGMENTS •

There are many people I would like to acknowledge in bringing this book into your hands, including those who help and support me personally, those who have specifically contributed to the writing of this book, and colleagues in the field of marital research who have helped develop the growing knowledge of commitment and marital dynamics that I find so valuable in bringing powerful ideas to couples.

In my personal life, there is no one I could thank any more strongly than my wonderful wife, Nancy. She loves me, challenges me, encourages me, and makes it possible for me to pursue projects such as this book to the fullest of my abilities. She not only made my thinking in this book better but also makes my whole life better, for which I am grateful. I am also inspired by my parents, who had their fifty-sixth wedding anniversary this past summer and who have one of those marriages most couples dream of. They are a lovely, wise, fun, and deeply dedicated couple. Their loving commitment is a model to me and to all who know them. They have influenced me greatly—and maybe even more than I can fully apprehend.

Four people were particularly helpful to me in bringing this manuscript together. First, Carol Whitely is a professional writer and editor who worked extensively with me to make this book come alive. She worked tirelessly and with great skill to improve the quality of what you read here. I greatly appreciate her input, writing, editing, and insights on various aspects of this work. Second, I would like to thank Natalie Jenkins. She has not only given me a great deal of insightful input about concepts but also directly contributed to this work by writing a piece on forgiveness for the chapter on grieving. She is a terrific writer and thinker, and this work is better for all of her input. Third, Galena Kline has my gratitude as well. She is a research colleague of mine at the University of Denver who is very involved in research on cohabitation and couple development. She works extensively with me and Dr. Howard Markman (my longtime friend and colleague) on a range of projects having to do with the prevention of marital distress and divorce and the understanding of couple development and commitment. She has mastered the research on cohabitation and wrote a thoughtful and thorough piece in Chapter Seven, where we discuss the research in this area and what it can mean for couples starting out together. Her work in the whole area of couple development will become highly influential in our field. Fourth, I want to thank Alan Rinzler, my editor on so many projects now. He's become a good friend and a trusted adviser. I find his wisdom and spirit to be of immense value, and if you find this book useful in your life, you have him to be thankful for, for without him it would simply not have come about.

This book is founded on the contributions of many others who struggle to better understand marriage and how to help couples. In particular, I thank my friend Howard Markman for over twenty-five years of friendship and productive engagement around ideas, research, and ways to help couples. He was one of the true pioneers to base advice for couples on sound science, and this book is in part an outgrowth of what he has done in this field and what has inspired me about the possibilities. There are a vast number of researchers whose work has been influential in my thoughts. I would like to specifically acknowledge the work of several who have played a very significant role in developing my thinking in various areas reflected throughout this book: Paul Amato, Norval Glenn, Mike Johnson, Steve Nock, Caryl Rusbult, and Linda Waite. These are giants in the field of marital research, and I am so fortunate to be able to draw on their work as I continually refine my own line of research on marriage.

I would also like to thank and acknowledge Gary Smalley. Gary has been so gracious to me in my work over the years. He's helped millions of couples through his books and tapes, but especially through his love, compassion, and wisdom. He is a great role model for all who desire to reach out and help others, and I admire him deeply.

Lastly, my thanks go to all of those named here as well as many others not named. No person's ideas come only from within him or her; rather they are developed by reading, talking, interacting, and thinking about the ideas of others. I have a rich group of friends and colleagues that set the foundation for the ideas I now bring to you.

Scott M. Stanley
Denver, Colorado

To Nancy,
Your loving commitment sustains me.
Until death parts us or the world ends,
I am yours and you are mine.

THE
POWER
OF
COMMITMENT

What is commitment, and what's so difficult, so scary about it? How can we better understand and appreciate the value and power of commitment? What does active commitment look like, and how is it different from the prevailing values of our culture? How can we actually make a commitment to another person and make it last—for a lifetime?

These are the core questions I address in this book. I have written it to challenge you to live out the fullness of commitment. I hope that the ideas you find here will both inspire you and give you practical, specific suggestions that will help you in your journey. But you're not going to find a quick and easy path to a great marriage here. In fact, you'll find that the journey to this wonderful, fulfilling state of union can be a real challenge at times. Just remember that although the risks can seem great, the rewards are greater.

Is This Book for You? Yes.

I've written this book for people who are interested in excelling in marriage. That includes you and all those who fit any of these descriptions:

- Couples who are doing great together in life and just want to make a good thing even better
- Couples who are committed to their marriages but who have lost their edge and want to be sharpened
- Couples who are engaged and planning their marriage and life ahead
- Singles who are looking toward their future and working

through how they think about marriage and the kind of
person they want to marry

- Couples who have lost their way and are really struggling,
and who want to recapture their dedication and devotion to
one another

Houston, We Have a Problem

Do you remember the famous line that *Apollo 13* astronaut Jack
Swigert made to Mission Control, announcing the ominous change
that had taken place in the crew's mission? "Houston, we have a
problem." (He actually said, "Houston, we've had a problem.") The
Apollo spacecraft lost most of its oxygen and a great deal of its electrical power when oxygen tank number 2 blew apart, taking tank
number 1 with it. The explosion ripped off the side of the service
module (the back part of the spacecraft), ending the hopes of the
astronauts to make it to the moon and instantly changing their goal
from exploration to survival.

Lest you be alarmed by that example, this book is not about
helping you merely to survive in marriage, but about helping you
to thrive in the richness of commitment. I use the story of the amazing feat of the *Apollo 13* team—those on the ground and those up
in space—because it's really a story of the power of commitment.
There was risk, but teamwork and dedication triumphed. And teamwork and dedication can triumph in marriage as well.

Some people are not that optimistic, though. With so many
painful, fragile, and failed marriages in evidence, many people have
come to fear that their personal shoot-for-the-moon journey will
end badly and off course, leaving them lost in space or gasping for
oxygen before they arrive where they had hoped—or blowing apart
dramatically, with fragments of their lives tumbling to the ground.

But other couples have never really doubted that they will make the journey and succeed, even if they encounter obstacles. Still others have already endured trauma to their ship and now are struggling to survive, to get through.

This book is for all those couples. This book is for you. No matter what your path and how high or low your risks, the book will show that the secrets to lifelong love lie in powerful acts of commitment that bring out the best in marriage—your marriage too.

But what do you want in life? Most people want a deep, lifelong, loving relationship. In fact, despite the very high divorce rate, most people want marriage, and they want their marriage to last.

Is that blind faith in the institution? Perhaps too often it is. Some expect marriage to work automatically—their own marriage, even—without giving enough thought to what really powers marital success. Others have become so cynical about marriage that they avoid it altogether, despite the ache in the heart for this deeper life and deeper commitment. We want it, but we fear it. The rocket on the launching pad might not look like it can make the trip. And the astronauts might be thinking, "I'm not getting into that little ship and blasting off for some faraway destination without a guarantee!"

Of course there are no guarantees. Statistically, marriage is as risky as space travel. Research suggests, however, that *not* being married may be even riskier, especially if you want the best shot at lifelong love. Nothing besides commitment in marriage brings the same benefits of health, economic stability, companionship, and even sexual satisfaction.[1] Living together without the commitment of marriage doesn't result in the same type or quality of relationship. There is real power in knowing that you're a team and that you can count on each other in the future.

I'm not going to make any guarantees that this book will ensure that you experience the contentment and happiness that come from committed love. But I do guarantee that the book is full of solid insights, inspiration, and tangible steps that can help you on your journey. There is plenty of good information and training here, based on the best ideas and latest research. However, the work is really up to you. You need to give your hard effort, your persistence, and your devotion. It's your journey, and you must get into the module—and stay. And that takes a lot of faith, but faith that you can live out with confidence.

Desiring Something Deeper

To get the most out of this book, you need to be in touch with one of two things: either your desire for a deep and lasting love or your fear of calling back to Mission Control with Jack Swigert's fateful words. To put it differently, either you can be an optimist who would like some practical guidance for the mission ahead, or you can be paralyzed by the fear that no ship can protect you from the cold dark of space. I'll take either. Either of these motives will drive you to get the most out of this book. In fact, you can be in a spaceship that has already come halfway apart. If that's your situation, there are ideas here that can help you do much more than simply survive.

I don't know each and every one of you personally, but I do know what you're looking for. I know because you wouldn't have read even this far if you weren't interested in lifelong, committed love. I also know because I believe that you and I and everyone else were created to deeply desire this type of relationship.

The Crisis: *Maybe* I Do

Ironically, the same decades that saw humans accomplish so much in space also saw humans unravel great things here on Earth. Divorce is just part of the story, but the story is a very significant one.

The divorce rate is incredibly high and, although it hasn't risen recently, it's not dropping greatly either. Young couples marrying for the first time today have only a 50 percent chance of going to the moon and back together. Others will make the whole journey, but only in a disintegrating ship, flying by the seat of their pants. Perhaps of even greater concern, more and more people are avoiding marriage altogether as they seek to avoid the pain of divorce. They think that if they never get into the rocket ship, there's no chance of blowing up in space.

Do you want to go? *"Maybe* I do" won't cut it as an answer. Marriage is too serious a business to hedge your bets by wanting to have a relationship without giving it your all. Great marriages require making real commitments. They require a firm "I do," not a *"Maybe* I do."

Of course, there is a kind of safety in never blasting off. There's also no chance of reaching that fulfilling place your heart yearns for. *"Maybe* I do" can't take you there and back. In fact, it won't even get you off the ground. If you were a candidate for space travel and the head of NASA asked you if you wanted to go to the moon, and you answered *"Maybe* I do," I'm pretty sure you'd never set foot near an actual spacecraft. I'm also pretty sure that that way of thinking and acting will keep you from ever accomplishing your most deeply desired mission in marriage.

Taking the Journey

This book is organized into three steps, each of which challenges you to learn about and act on commitment:

> *Step One: Understanding the Importance of Commitment.* This section looks at what commitment is, how it develops, and how it relates to our deepest desires in life.
>
> *Step Two: Battling the Myths That Undermine Commitment.* This step challenges the myths that many people believe and that compromise true commitment in marriage.
>
> *Step Three: Building Your Future with the Power of Commitment.* The final section focuses on the value of having a vision for your marriage. It includes strategies for fostering deeper acceptance, investing for the long term, and regaining the deeper dedication you once had.

Scientific Research and Insights from Scripture

Throughout this book, you will see that I rely a great deal on scientific research, including research by eminent marital scholars and colleagues, including Dr. Howard Markman, a colleague at the Center for Marital and Family Studies at the University of Denver. Much of our work has been supported by the National Institute of Mental Health. *Boring*, you might think. No. *Exciting!* You will see. I admit I am a research geek, but there are studies that have provided us with amazingly interesting points to think about—ideas you might never have thought about otherwise. But even the obvious points are important to read, because they show that a lot about great marriages simply makes sense.

Here are two examples of the kind of research I include. Research by Sarah Whitton, Howard Markman, and me shows that how men feel about making the regular sacrifices good marriages require depends on how strongly they want a future with their mate. Those men who are less committed to their partner for the future are less likely to sacrifice in the here and now without resenting it. The situation is very different for women, who seem to be willing to sacrifice for their partners whether or not they are fully committed. In another study, we found that couples who lived together before marriage tended to have husbands who were less committed than other husbands, even after marriage. There is no such difference for women. We'll look at what these and other important findings mean for marriage and for you.

In addition to research findings, this book will also include another source of wisdom and inspiration: you'll find stirring passages from the Bible to highlight core teachings and points about commitment and priorities in marriage. Even if you're not religiously inclined, I think you'll find the passages to be meaningful. They're included not to be preachy but because they convey remarkable wisdom. If you *are* religiously inclined, especially from a background that appreciates Scripture, I think the passages will bring key points alive for you on a deeper, spiritual level.

But now it's time to continue your journey. You have already begun acting on your commitment just by starting this book. But don't stop there. Read through the entire book. Think about the questions asked in exercises and take the action steps suggested at the end of each chapter. The power of commitment does not come from good ideas and positive thoughts alone, but from love put into action. That's the path to the greatest contentment and satisfaction in marriage. So suit up, fuel up, and get ready to lift off.

Understanding the Importance of Commitment

To love at all is to be vulnerable. Love anything and your heart will certainly be wrung and possibly broken. If you want to make sure of keeping it intact, you must give your heart to no one, not even an animal. Wrap it carefully round with hobbies and little luxuries; avoid all entanglements; lock it up safe in the casket or coffin of your selfishness. But in that casket—safe, dark, motionless, airless—it will change. It will not be broken; it will become unbreakable, impenetrable, irredeemable.

C. S. LEWIS

Goal of Step One: The goal of this step is to help you understand the depth of what commitment is really about in order to lay a foundation for the ideas in the rest of the book.

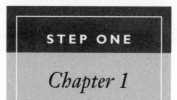

STEP ONE

Chapter 1

Understanding Commitment in a "Maybe I Do" World

To have and to hold
from this day forward,
for better or for worse,
for richer, for poorer,
in sickness and in health,
to love and to cherish;
and I promise to be faithful to you,
forsaking all others,
until death do us part.

As reflected in these beautiful vows, commitment is at the core of a deeply fulfilling marriage. Most of us dream of journeying through life with that special person who knows how to make us smile, help us believe in ourselves, hold us close, and treasure us always. While we hope that commitment will take us to the mountaintops, we know that it can take us through deep valleys too. The road to lasting love takes dedication and determination, and I feel it is only fair to warn you that this book is not for the faint of heart. It will take you to the inner regions of your heart as we look together at the importance of commitment and how to maintain and deepen your commitment over the lifelong course of your marriage.

True commitment is far more than saying "until death do us part." That vow reflects the sanctity of marriage, but it doesn't guarantee that you will have a lifelong happy marriage. This book can help you go far beyond simply *staying together* to really *being together* in the full mystery and magic of marriage.

The Way Forward

Over the course of these pages, I am going to provide important information that will help you understand the concept of commitment. In this chapter, I focus on what current marital research and theory say about commitment, including a look at the trends in our culture that make it less likely than ever that people will fulfill their deepest desires for lasting love. After laying that foundation, we'll go deeper in the second chapter, looking at the nature and origin of the powerful desire to be fully known and accepted in marriage. We'll do this by studying Adam and Eve, the first couple with deep desires and the first to experience the fear of rejection.

In the middle section of this book, we will look at major myths related to commitment—myths that many people believe but that take lasting, committed love further out of the realm of possibility. We'll look at the following:

- The myth that you can have it all
- The myth that loved ones will wait forever to be a priority in your life
- The myth that the grass is greener
- The myth that love is all about you and what you can get from your mate
- Myths about children and divorce, cohabitation, and soul mates

In each one of these areas, what you believe can affect how you choose to live your life. Each myth has the potential to erode your chances for a great marriage, and each represents beliefs that you need to battle in order to achieve a great marriage.

In the last section of the book, we will focus on three powerful themes. The first is about the importance of having a vision for your marriage (and life). A proper vision propels you to accomplish great things—and a lasting, loving marriage is a great accomplishment in life. The second theme involves coping with the sense of loss that often comes hand in hand with true commitment. Commitment requires your giving up some paths for the sake of the road you choose to travel, and sometimes you will feel a sense of loss about the paths not taken. The final theme is about the importance of acting on the long-term view. We will look at how to invest fully in your marriage so that you can continue reaping its blessings in the years to come.

The last chapter in the book is not for everyone. It's for those of you who are really struggling, who have lost your way and need to get back on the right path. In that chapter we will look at ways to recapture what has been lost so that you and your partner can live together with hope and happiness.

Research and Religious Bases of This Book

Much of what you'll find in this book is based on solid research. In various research centers, such as the Center for Marital and Family Studies at the University of Denver, where Dr. Howard Markman and I lead a team of excellent social scientists, researchers study a wide range of elements that help us understand how great marriages come about and what causes some couples to struggle. These elements include communication, happiness, family backgrounds, expectations, problems, commitment, and conflict styles.

But I don't just draw on research that my colleagues and I conduct. There are many studies that teach us about commitment, and many important points in the book are well founded both in sound research and insights from the Scriptures. If you wish to learn more about some of the topics I discuss, please check the notes organized by chapter at the back of the book.

Now, to start giving shape to the substance of the book, let's meet two couples on their wedding day.

Dreams and Fears

The big day had finally arrived. The wedding had been carefully planned and everything was going smoothly—except that Lisa didn't feel so smooth inside. As her mother helped her straighten her veil, Lisa whispered, "What if I'm not making the right choice?" Although she could have been expressing wedding-day jitters, Lisa really did have doubts. Although she and Steven had dated for four years, and no one else had come along whom she liked as well, her parents had divorced when Lisa was seven. She remembered the pain of their separation as if it were yesterday. That event, and the preceding years of turmoil and conflict, had left her skeptical that any marriage could really work—at least over many years.

While Lisa wondered whether she was doing the right thing, her mother tried to comfort her: "Honey, you don't have to worry so much. Remember, you can always come back home if things don't work out with Steven." To her mother's surprise, Lisa burst into sad and anxious sobs. Lisa didn't really want to hear that there was a lifeboat; she knew she could go home if she had to. She wanted to hear that it was possible to have a lifelong, happy marriage with Steven. She had grave doubts, and she wanted them to go away.

Through her tears, Lisa said to her mother, "Mom, thank you for trying to reassure me. But I desperately want to know that it's really possible for this to work, that it's not a fairy tale. I am so afraid that we don't have what it takes, but I want our marriage to last all my life. That just doesn't seem realistic, does it?"

Well, does it? What do you think? Lisa's parents had divorced, but her mother told her that things could be different for her and Steven. She didn't need to end up unhappy in her marriage. She didn't have to end up divorced. She gave Lisa all the reassurance she was hoping for. Lisa managed a smile, but she still agonized: "Do we know how to live out a commitment over many years?"

Soon after asking that question, Lisa married Steven, with all her desires and doubts intact. She desperately hoped that she and Steven would remain faithful in their dedication to each other for the rest of their lives, that they would stick, but she knew that they could end up just stuck together for decades.

On the same day, Jeremy and Suzanne were getting married across town. It was a day of anticipation and rejoicing for both of their families. In one room of the church, Jeremy was with his father and his brother Chris, who was Jeremy's best man. Suzanne was with her mother, her sister, and Jeremy's mother getting ready in another part of the church.

As Jeremy's father and brother sat in the room chatting with him, Jeremy closed the door. He said, "I have something to say that I want you both to hear." Jeremy stood before father and brother and went on: "The commitment that I am making today is sacred. I am committing myself to Suzanne for life, for all that I am and can be in this marriage. I am asking both of you to hold me accountable to this commitment. I am asking you to push me to love her in the fullest measure for all of my life."

Jeremy's father hugged his son, and the three men vowed to support one another in living out their commitments. It was a powerful moment that none of the men would forget.

As you can see, Jeremy's concept of marriage was very different from Lisa's, but their desire was similar. His parents had demonstrated commitment to each other by showing their love in the ups and downs of their life. That was the model that Jeremy brought to his marriage. By watching his parents he had inherited a clear sense of the sanctity of the wedding commitment.

After Jeremy spoke to his father and brother, he and Suzanne said their vows together—the traditional vows that opened this chapter. Before they said them, they had pondered the words, and they meant every one of them. But would making these public vows be enough? It would be if they follow through.

The two couples in these stories began their wedded life with similar hopes and dreams. But they had very different levels of confidence that they could really fulfill their vows of marriage in a full, happy life together.

Reality Is Rough

Here in the United States, 40 to 50 percent of young couples who marry for the first time will eventually divorce.[1] Many will end their marriages within the first few years of their wedding day. In contrast, most older couples have a very low risk of divorce. These couples truly married for life and have made it through some tough trials. But even though the divorce rate for these older couples will be nowhere near 40 to 50 percent, the number of divorces for older couples has gone up as well.

Where do the promises of marriage go? Most couples start out wanting the "until death do us part" kind of marriage. Just as important, all couples I have met want that "to love and to cherish, to have and to hold" kind of marriage as well. Most of us get married because we believe we have found the special person with whom we can have all these things. Although couples may increasingly fear that divorce is a possibility, I am convinced that most newlyweds start out believing that it will be other couples who will divorce, not them. It's hard for them to believe that their love will not be cherished and deepen over time. They think, *Our commitment can't possibly erode like that of so many other couples.*

As divorce has become far more common, the level of confidence that people have in marriage has gone down. This is widely believed by researchers to be the reason that young people are putting off marriage until an older and older age, that they are more likely than ever before to have children without being married, that they feel they must be financially established prior to marrying, and that they enter into prenuptial agreements. People are hedging their bets because after all, you can't be too sure about marriage anymore—or so these people believe.

This crisis of confidence in marriage affects many people, and children of divorced parents most of all. As we'll see in Chapter Seven, those whose parents divorced are more likely to come into their own adult relationships anxious about whether they will last and more accepting of the possibility of divorce. The lack of confidence also compounds the risks for couples in which one or both spouses' parents divorced—the concern that commitment may not last actually makes it more likely that it will not last.[2] The worry that marriage won't work out becomes a self-fulfilling prophecy.

How and Why Commitment Develops

When you become deeply attached to another and fall in love, you may enter a period of anxiety about the future of the relationship. The anxiety becomes greatest after you have experienced intense satisfaction but before the two of you have committed to be together. From a psychological standpoint, various forms of commitment develop in order to make this anxiety go away. It's scary to be in love with someone when you don't know whether the person is going to remain in your life.

There are many incremental steps in forming commitment. When teenagers pledge to go steady, that's a form of commitment. When teenagers give a "steady" a class ring to wear or hang around the neck, they are pledging a higher level of commitment. Hold it! Stop a second and think about what you just read. Teenagers don't do those things anymore, which I think is very meaningful. There used to be all kinds of symbols couples had that spoke of their deepening commitment, but virtually none of them is widely visible any longer.

These old practices were important because they were public emblems between two young people that communicated "you are mine and I am yours." Even though these commitments were often immature in many ways—teenagers were making them, and they were not meant to be full, lifelong commitments—they were right for the dating couple's level of development, and they functioned as mature commitments do: to get rid of the anxiety about loss.

The force of such emblems of commitment, simple as they are, affects both the internal and the external parts of relationships. Internally, they communicate a sense of allegiance, that "you can count on me to be here for you." Externally, they convey a sense of exclusivity. Each person is publicly identified as "belonging" to the other, at least for a time. These messages have many levels of meaning, but the root of them is "You have me; you can relax." When given to a partner in marriage, a full, clear commitment embodies both messages—*you can count on me* and *others take note, we are a couple going through life together.*

I believe that the old emblems of developing commitment have gone the way of the dinosaurs because commitment itself has been under steady attack since the early 1960s. What has replaced them? For many couples, cohabitation has become one of the few tangible steps they believe reflects their growing commitment and the desire for security. As we'll see in detail in Chapter Seven, the problem with taking this step is that cohabitation outside of marriage does not reduce risks for couples; in fact, decades of research show just the opposite. Furthermore, it's a step that's actually associated, on average, with lower, not higher, levels of commitment in men toward women.

Real commitment has real power to turn a good relationship into a great marriage. It lays a firm foundation for the attachment between partners. Without that security, partners don't feel safe, and they will not invest as much in the future.

Safety: The Foundation of a Great Marriage

In our research, I and my colleague Howard Markman have come to believe that the most essential elements of a great marriage are three types of safety:[3]

1. *Safety in the connection.* Feeling emotionally safe, feeling that you will be supported and accepted. It allows you, for example, to talk openly and well about key issues.
2. *Personal safety.* Feeling safe from physical or emotional harm or intimidation.
3. *Safety in commitment.* Feeling secure that you mutually support each other, work as a team, and have a clear future together.

The focus of this book is the third type of safety; I will show both its power and how to develop it to the fullest in *your* marriage. As I'll show you in the next chapter, however, through a look at Adam and Eve, the first type of safety is what we all long for most deeply. Yet the first type needs the foundation of the third type in order to reach full potential in marriage. Of course, personal safety is crucial as well, and commitment when there is ongoing danger should be avoided. If you are in danger in your marriage or relationship, this book will not provide the help you need. I strongly encourage you to seek outside help to take wise steps to become safe.

Although most people still long for greater acceptance and a deeper connection, they have begun to disconnect that longing from the need to develop security in commitment. The erosion of commitment in marriage has actually made it more and more difficult for people to achieve their deepest desires in life.

Exercising Your Commitment

How safe do you feel in your marriage or relationship regarding the commitment you and your partner have made to each other?

> If you feel anxious about the commitment, think about what makes you feel that way and ask your partner to do the same. Then discuss what you would both need to do to strengthen the feeling of safety in your relationship.

Troubling Trends

There are also many trends that make it less likely that young people will achieve their desire for lasting love and security. Consider these facts:

- Over many years, the University of Michigan's "Monitoring Our Future" survey tracked teens' answers to the question of whether or not they agreed with the statement, "Most people will have fuller and happier lives if they choose legal marriage rather than staying single or just living with someone."[4] In the late 1970s, 39 percent of girls and 38 percent of boys said yes. By the late 1990s, however, 38 percent of boys still said yes, but only 28 percent of girls said yes. The survey has shown that most young people do expect to eventually marry.[5]
- An overwhelming majority (94 percent) of never-married singles agree that "when you marry you want your spouse to be your soul mate, first and foremost."[6] (We will focus on this point in Chapter Seven.)
- Less than half (42 percent) of single young adults believe that it is important to find a spouse who shares their own religion.[7]
- The greater portion of children born to women ages twenty to twenty-four in the United States are now born to

unmarried women—thus reflecting the degree to which child rearing is becoming disconnected from marriage.[8]

- When asked "How likely do you think it is that you would stay married to the same person for life?" only 61 percent of teens in 1995 thought this was "very likely."[9] (To learn more about these and other trends, which are reported on regularly in publications of the National Marriage Project, please see their website: http://marriage.rutgers.edu/.)

As these statements show, young people don't have great confidence that lasting marriage is possible. They are also unsure of the benefits marriage actually provides. At the same time, however, they want marriage as much as ever and have extremely high expectations for the kind of partner they want to find (a soul mate).

The pessimism that research uncovers about what teens feel is possible and what matters, combined with their continuing desire for a great marriage, is stunning. I am especially concerned about the growing tendency of young women to think that marriage won't matter much for them in the face of growing evidence that women get the best from men when men make the commitment to marry them. Along with sociologist Steve Nock, I believe that committing to a future with a woman, especially in marriage, appears to change men—it draws them to invest more, sacrifice more, and take on more responsibility.[10] I am not saying that marriage can turn a bad man into a good man. I am saying that there is plenty of evidence that marriage, on average, makes most men better men and better partners to their wives. If our culture continues to erode marriage, I believe it will ultimately be bad for both men and women, but women will suffer more, and sooner. You can read more about my specific thoughts about men and women and commitment in marriage by going to our website (www.PREPinc.com) and downloading the paper entitled "What Is It with Men and Commitment, Anyway?" on the Policy Issues and Marital Research page.

Two Kinds of Commitment

What are the ways in which commitment is expressed in the warp and woof of a life together? Consider these two statements and what is reflected in each:

> "Mary sure is committed to that project."
> "Bob committed to that project; he can't back out now."

The different kinds of commitment reflected in these two statements profoundly affect your marriage. Michael Johnson, a researcher at Penn State University, noted this distinction some years ago. His theories and mine have diverged a bit over the years, but we both continue to emphasize the importance of this most basic distinction.[11]

In the terms I use in my work, the first statement reflects commitment as *dedication*, and the second reflects commitment as *constraint*. *Dedication* implies an internal state of devotion to a person or project. It conveys the sense of a forward-moving, motivating force, one based on thoughtful decisions you have made to give your best effort. *Constraint* entails a sense of obligation. It refers to factors that would be costs if the present course were abandoned. Whereas dedication is a force drawing you forward, constraint is a force pushing you from behind. When you combine the two, as Bill Coffin, an expert in the prevention of marital and family problems, has noted, it's like epoxy glue. Mixing the two components gives married couples a superstrong bond.

Research has shown that couples who maintain and act on dedication are more connected, happier, and more open with each other.

That's because dedicated partners show their commitment in the following very specific ways, which we will look at throughout this book:

- They think more like a team, with a strong orientation toward "us" and "we."
- They make their partner and marriage a high priority.
- They protect their relationship from attraction to others.
- They sacrifice for one another without resentment.
- They invest of themselves in building a future together—they have a long-term view.

Those who lose dedication and have only constraints will either be together but miserable (hardly a pleasant situation for the couple or their children) or come apart. The loss of dedication represents the loss of the will to try, the loss of the sense of "us," and the loss of the actions that protect a marriage over time. Furthermore, a marriage without dedication is a marriage without passion. I don't mean romantic passion, though that could be part of it. I mean a marriage devoid of life. I want to help you steer clear of that. This book is mostly about the dedication side of commitment: what it looks like, what it does, and how it keeps the two of you connected and contented in life. Let's take a look at how the forces of dedication and constraint work.

I Signed Up for Adventure!

Jason was up late one night, surfing the channels on TV. He was fresh out of high school—an eighteen-year-old with his life ahead of him. However, he was not certain where he wanted his life to take him. But that night he found the answer in a U.S. Marine Corps commercial: "Be one of the few and the proud." He thought to himself, *Those guys look strong. They look proud. I bet they have an exciting life.*

Jason thought about it for weeks, with the idea of joining the marines steadily growing inside him. Finally he got up his nerve and went to talk to the recruiter, who painted a picture that might not have been entirely realistic: exotic lands, important duties, choices, and, most important, adventure. Jason signed up on the spot. Though basic training turned out to be pretty tedious, combat training proved to be more exciting. Jason thought he had found what he was looking for.

When he completed his training, Jason got his orders and shipped out to an island in the Indian Ocean he had never heard of. *No big deal*, he thought. *This is an adventure.* Well, six weeks later, he was into his fifth week of guard duty on a wharf for navy supply ships. It was not exciting work. It was not an adventure. It was pure, hot drudgery. *I may be one of the few*, he thought, *but I'm not so proud at the moment. I did not sign up for this!*

Most of us don't talk to a recruiter before we get married. However, like Jason entering the corps, many of us start out in marriage with unrealistic expectations, or we pay attention only to the really wonderful-sounding stuff. When he signed up for the marines, Jason was filled with a sense of dedication. I say a "sense" because his dedication was not very strong at that time—it was really more like *potential* dedication. But his initial dedication carried him happily through the commitment of signing up, basic training, and combat training.

What was enough to see Jason through the early stages of joining the marines was not enough to see him through the hard duties that carried no particular prospects for glory and adventure. His dedication began to drain away. He was still committed, but he was no longer a free man. He could not go to the staff sergeant and say something like, "Sir, this has been an interesting time so far, but I don't think I'm really into being a marine anymore. I'd like to be excused."

Jason came to know the full force of constraint. Although he did talk with the chaplain about his dilemma, he could not simply get up and walk away. (Actually, he could, but the Marine Corps takes a rather dim view of that as I understand it.) Mostly he felt aware of what the costs would be if he left.

Jason took on his commitment with the force of dedication. It was his choice. He did not have to do it. Despite that, when he was faced with unmet and unrealistic expectations, deep disappointment grew. Although he was no less constrained before his dedication left him, he was not very aware of his constraint until then. Once he became aware of it, he realized, *I cannot leave, or else I'll go to federal prison.* He felt trapped. And trapped he was. What was he to do?

Jason made it through his three-year commitment to the marines. The awareness of his constraint led him to make the wise choice to embrace dedication again, and at that point his dedication was more informed and more mature. He realized that he had made the choice to join the marines, so he would do his best with it. *After all*, he thought, *as long as I am in this boat, I might as well quit shooting holes in the bottom and learn to sail.*

It was a good attitude, and with that attitude Jason's assignments got better. As he discovered, sometimes all of life hinges on a positive shift in perspective. To put it in terms a marine would love, *When you hit the beach, you can sit there and get pinned down and shot up, or you can take the hill. Go for the hill. Go for the higher ground.*

After fulfilling his duties with honor, Jason left the corps and went back to his hometown.

Committing to a Choice

When Laura graduated from high school, she, like Jason, had no idea what she wanted to do for a career. She did know, though, that she wanted to go to college. After agonizing over the choice, she decided to go to a university in another state. But she wasn't sure she had made a good decision. She was afraid she'd miss her family.

As it turned out, she loved the school she had chosen. She also was able to see her family often, because her roommate had a car and liked to go home with Laura for occasional weekends.

But close to the end of her sophomore year, Laura still had no idea what sort of career she wanted. She had always enjoyed photography, but her parents had told her it would be hard to make a living as a photographer. So she decided to major in business and perhaps become an accountant. Her father was an accountant, and he seemed to like his work and was always very busy. But the decision was hard, and Laura worried that she was always going to have trouble making decisions. But accounting it was.

At the start of her senior year, she met a new classmate who had just done a summer internship as a photographer at a local magazine. It sounded great. It sounded exciting. And suddenly Laura was filled with doubts. She should have majored in photography and followed her interest. Compared to photography and magazine work, accounting seemed like a mistake.

When Laura dedicated herself to her choice of accounting, she had put aside her interest in photography. Now that interest was back. The constraint that made her choose accounting instead of photography began to feel like a noose. But she was so close to graduation. She couldn't start over at this point. And if she said she planned to make photography her career, her parents would worry.

Laura took some time to think. And the more she thought, the more she realized that she had made a choice she needed to stay with. It was the right thing to do on several levels.

But she still felt a sense of loss. *I could have become a magazine or newspaper photographer,* she thought. *I think it would have been fantastic. I won't be able to do that now.* But she also realized that being a photographer might not be the right career for the kind of life she wanted. For instance, she might have to travel a lot, rather than be close to her family, and there might not be many magazines to work for where she wanted to live.

She also realized that she could still pursue her interest in photography. It wouldn't be her career, but she could take photos for herself, and maybe attend some classes later on. That made her feel better and helped her recommit herself to a career in business. And after thinking some more, she decided that the future was probably going to continue to be full of choices and that from time to time she might mourn the "road not taken." But that was OK. It was part of life.

Déjà Vu

After Jason got out of the marines at the age of twenty-one, he decided to go to college. While he had been a marine, he had found that he really liked to work with computers and was very good at it. His superiors had caught on to his skill and asked him to complete a variety of tasks using high-tech equipment and computers.

Jason applied to and was accepted at a college where he could study computer science. It was there, in a computer lab, that he met Laura. She was the same age, but three years ahead of him in her course work. He thought she was beautiful, and he learned she wasn't seeing anyone. She thought he was good looking too, but she did wonder about his short hair. He explained that he had grown to like short hair when he had been a marine, and told her a bit about his life in the corps. Laura thought the ex-marine was intriguing. Jason thought Laura was great.

They fell deeply in love. As they dated, they learned many things about each other. They both had a love of the outdoors. They also had similar church backgrounds, coming from families with strong faith in the basics. After dating for nine months, Jason asked Laura *the* question. She said, "Yes." Seven months later, they were married in a traditional ceremony at the church near campus, with a wealth of approving friends and family in attendance. Both were ecstatic. It was a fine day.

Now let's fast-forward. Six years after the wedding day, Jason and Laura were struggling. She was working for a large accounting firm and enjoyed her work. He was likewise doing fine, working on computer networks at a local company that took good care of its employees. All his colleagues liked him, and he was in line for a promotion.

Things were not so good at home, however. It was far harder to deal with their relationship than either Jason or Laura had imagined. Laura thought, *No one told me about how hard this could be.* Going into the marriage, she hadn't realized it could be tough. She hadn't known anyone who struggled much in marriage, at least from what she'd been able to see. Though not perfect, her parents' marriage was delightful.

But time went on, and Jason and Laura had a child, a girl named Kristi. She grew into an adorable three-year-old and was no problem to them at all. Both of them loved being parents and found that they could have positive times together when they played with Kristi.

But otherwise, things were unpleasant. The two argued frequently. Neither had very good skills for handling conflict, so many of the arguments ended up with Laura yelling and Jason pulling back into himself. The arguments could be about anything, it seemed, but most were about money, which is typical of most couples. When they talked, as often as not it was an argument, and that is a major danger sign for a marriage over time.[12] They rarely went out or did anything fun, and their sexual relationship cooled.

They drifted. They lost the sense of being friends—another sign that the relationship was seriously off track. Neither tried hard any longer to meet the needs of the other.

Déjà vu struck them both. Laura remembered the day when it hit her that life was going to be a series of choices, with occasional grief attached. Now she realized that her choice of Jason was one that had grief attached. Similarly, it struck Jason that once again he didn't have what he had expected. It wasn't the Marine Corps, but his marriage was going forward because of constraint, not dedication. And his commitment to Laura was for more than three years! He felt deeply discouraged and cheated: *This isn't what I signed up for*, he thought. Both he and Laura felt stuck.

Jason was no longer devoted to Laura in the way he had been, and he knew it. Likewise, Laura was just hanging on. *This happens to other people, not to me*, she said to herself. She and Jason were committed, but it was more from constraint than dedication. Laura had greater dedication than Jason, and she did try to reach out to him in some ways, such as by talking about key issues. Unfortunately, he thought she wanted to fight, so he ignored her.

Constraint doesn't make for deep commitment; without dedication, it merely it keeps you going in the same direction you're already headed. That can be very important during rough times, but it's not enough for experiencing what you most hoped for in your marriage.

Laura didn't feel quite as trapped as Jason, but she did feel betrayed—betrayed by Jason for not being who she had thought he was and betrayed by herself for believing *her* marriage would be different. Both wondered about divorce, but neither considered it much of an option. They had a crucial choice to make.

Where Laura and Jason would land all depended on what they chose to do—and choosing to do nothing would keep them stuck at best. How could they recapture and protect their dedication? More important to our discussion, how could they have prevented losing it?

? Did You Know . . .

Various researchers and I have been studying the factors that produce greater constraint in marriage,[13] and the following list includes the key factors. A way to understand each of them is that, all other things being equal, any person who experiences a greater number of them will be more constrained in his or her marriage. These factors are also associated with the costs of ending a marriage, which is an essential part of the concept of constraint commitment.

- *Social pressure* refers to whether or not friends, family, and community will disapprove if you end your marriage.
- *Morality of divorce* refers to the degree to which you believe that divorce is a wrong choice in most circumstances.
- *Concern for the welfare of the children* refers to the degree to which you believe your children would be harmed by divorce.

- *Financial limitations and losses* refer to how (and if) your
  lifestyle outside of the marriage would change and if it would
  be worse financially, or not tolerable.
- *Termination procedures,* coined by researcher Michael Johnson,
  refer to how difficult the steps would be to end the marriage.
- *Alternative quality* refers to your sense of the quality of your
  life apart from your mate and all other dimensions.

These forces can encourage struggling couples to remain
committed to their marriage even when they don't want to be.
But they are equally present in the lives of happy, dedicated couples. Constraints naturally increase over time in marriage and
help couples keep their marriages from coming apart when foul
winds blow. Whether you are fairly happily married or struggling, the key is to move beyond having only constraints and back
to a life of dedication.

Jason and Laura were in the same troubled waters that too many
couples have sailed. Their dedication, along with their joy and attachment, had seriously eroded. Each was aware of how much he or she
hated the idea of divorce. Jason was also thinking about how mad
his family would be if he left Laura. Laura was fearful about what it
would mean to Kristi if her marriage failed. And both Laura and
Jason knew that each of them could not make ends meet without
the other. Basically, they were in deep trouble—stuck together, but
not necessarily sticking together. They had enough constraint that
they *would* stay together. The really big question was whether they
would reengage and act on dedication.

Choice: The Root of the Matter

As you will see throughout this book, virtually every aspect of commitment revolves around the issue of choice. Commitment fundamentally requires making a choice to give up other choices. That's stating it simply, but couples who thrive rather than merely survive are those who consistently make the right choices throughout life. Those choices confirm your commitment, protect what you have built so far, and allow you to build toward the future.

It's choice that really makes commitment so powerful, giving you the ability to do things, daily and weekly, that go a long way toward creating a happy future in your marriage. But beware. You cannot make and keep commitments if you are unwilling to make choices among your options. Meditate for a moment on this simple verse from Solomon:

> He who observes the wind will not sow,
> and he who regards the clouds will not reap
> [Ecclesiastes 11:4 (ESV)].

To use Solomon's words, we have become a society of wind watchers. Wind watchers never plant because the conditions just don't seem quite right. They never bring in the crop because *it looks like* rain. Hesitancy is Solomon's target in this verse. People who hesitate to act—who don't choose to act—often end up with nothing, or at least a lot less than they could have had. Not making clear, committed choices in life is a guaranteed pathway to emptiness.

But what if I make a commitment prematurely? you may be thinking. People can make commitments prematurely, and suffer greatly for doing so. For example, they may marry someone they have known for only a short period of time, and that's usually very unwise.

However, I think a bigger danger is that many people in our culture resist making any clear commitment because they fear they will lose out on something else that might show up. They think, *What if my soul mate comes along a year after I marry this other person? I could lose out.*

"Maybe I Do" Commitments

If wind watchers enter marriage at all, they do so with a *maybe I do* commitment, not a fully expressed commitment that clearly says "I do." Our "maybe I do" culture encourages us to do that, to hedge our bets and protect ourselves rather than take any risks. But "maybe I do" will not get you where your soul longs to be.

The deepest, richest blessings in marriage are not guaranteed by your commitment, because not everything in life and love is under your control—but your commitment is. So jump all the way in, make the choice to give your relationship your all. Even though contrary winds will come your way, you can choose your course well and apply all your effort to reaching your destination. This book will show you how.

KEY COMMITMENT ACTIONS

- Ponder the two kinds of commitment and discuss them with your mate.
- Resolve to deepen dedication in your marriage and ask your partner to do the same.
- Resolve to give your relationship your all.

Now add and take your own action steps to strengthen your commitment even more:

_____

_____

_____

Chapter 2

The Deepest Desires
of the Heart

W hat do you desire in the deeper parts of your being? That is the subject of this chapter, though we won't be looking into it at length. That's because I don't think we should try to pin down the deepest mysteries of marriage or try to explain them in simple words. I'm going to write about them briefly, but it's more important to reflect on them. I'm going to use the story of Adam and Eve to highlight what I think most people really want and hope for in marriage.

My goal in looking at Adam and Eve in this chapter is to get at some deeper truths about marriage. However, for those of you who are less religious or less familiar with Scripture, I truly hope that this approach does not put you off. If it does, you can, of course, skip this chapter and move onto the next—as this is certainly the most scripturally focused chapter in the entire book. But I want you to know that I have tried to raise these themes in a way that just about anyone can appreciate, no matter what their background. For those of you who do have a background in reading and thinking about Scripture, my hope is that you will encounter fresh perspective from familiar ground.

As I said in the first chapter, there are many reasons to be pessimistic about the institution of marriage when you look at current trends. On the other hand, there is one major reason to hope that marriage as a way of life will not disappear: we humans desire to be deeply known and loved. To be loved in that way, however, we must commit ourselves to our marriage, a point that is made clear in the teachings about Adam and Eve.

Our First Couple

No matter what your religious or spiritual background, you are most likely familiar with the story of Adam and Eve. This first marriage couple were the first to experience how great the distance can be between the promise of ultimate love and soul-jarring rejection.

When we look in Genesis (1–3) we read how God created one thing, then another, then another—all in a very orderly manner and all to perfection. And we read that He saw that all of it was good. Then Adam was created, and God said that it was not good for him to be alone.

I sometimes joke that it's just never a good idea to leave a man alone for very long. But God was saying that what he had created was not yet all it could be. So God created Eve.

The missing ingredient that made the difference between things being not good and things being good was the woman God created, Eve. Whole books have been written about all the meaningful lessons in the story of Adam and Eve, but my focus here is the lesson about intimacy and commitment.

When Eve was created, Adam was very pleased. Following that, we read:

> Therefore a man shall leave his father and his mother and hold fast to his wife, and they shall become one flesh. And the man and his wife were both naked and were not ashamed [Genesis 2:24–25 ESV].

Let's look first at the last verse, at the concept of being *naked and not ashamed*. There are few other short phrases in the Bible that are so packed with meaning, because it speaks to the deepest desires for connection and fulfillment that most people feel. Take a moment now to think about what thoughts and feelings those words stir in you.

Then think about this: Adam's first reaction to what he sees and knows about Eve is focused on the physical. The word *naked* in verse 25 puts emphasis on the physical, and it is really the physical union of man and woman in marriage that illustrates one of the most amazing concepts of all: unity through diversity. The physical, passionate union between husband and wife is a tangible symbol of our deep desire to be joined to another, reflecting the profound marital math wherein one plus one equals a new type of one.

Although the focus of this book is not the physical side of marriage—others have covered this ground well, such as Tim Gardner in a book I highly recommend, *Sacred Sex*[1]—I want to call attention to the fact that the physical union between Adam and Eve is profoundly fundamental to the teachings presented about marriage. Unity from diversity in marriage is symbolized in the act of sexual connection. This has many implications, not the least of which is the fact that sexuality is an area of great, maybe the greatest, vulnerability

Sexuality's ability to touch us so deeply can be both a blessing and a curse. It's a curse when people attempt to experience the ultimate in sexual connection outside the framework of marriage. Research consistently shows that people are most satisfied sexually within the context of commitment in marriage,[2] and it is within marriage that the conditions are most favorable for being deeply touched and accepted.

for people. It touches us so deeply that it's no wonder it has the enormous power it does in our lives.

But the passage about Adam and Eve speaks not only to their physical relationship but to the level of their desire and connection—they are somehow in a naked state without shame. There is something deeper going on here, beyond the tangible and the physical.

I do not think there is one simple answer about what naked and unashamed means—the words are so profound and mysterious that they are very hard to explain in words. But let's make an attempt. Adam and Eve became one, or joined, as the passage says in English, without any self-consciousness or fear. They felt completely safe because they had no fear of the possibility of rejection. They had no reason to be guarded. Both Adam and Eve knew the wonder of being fully seen yet fully accepted as well as desired by and fulfilled in the other.

Choice and Permanence in Commitment

In addition to learning about naked-without-shame love, we also learn from the passage about Adam and Eve quite a lot about commitment. The passage tells us that commitment in marriage fundamentally involves *choice*, and that some choices will be hard.

When you get married, your commitment implies that you must leave some things behind. In the Genesis passage, we see that *a man shall leave his father and mother.* The full force of this passage is easier to appreciate if you bear in mind that the Torah (the first five books of the Bible) promotes a very high level of respect for parents. The priority you put on your commitment to your mate is to exceed the very high priority you give to your parents.

In addition to pointing out the fact of choice, the passage from Genesis also portrays the picture of *permanence* in marriage in the words "a man . . . shall hold fast to his wife." The word for "hold fast" in this passage is the Hebrew word *dabaq*, which means "to adhere," "to cling," or "to stick." Unfortunately, for too many, the image of commitment in marriage—of being joined or held fast— is more one of being stuck than of sticking. But that falls far short of what is being described in the story of the creation of marriage, far short of the deep intertwining of two lives in the fullness of life.

Such joining or cleaving is not for entrapping but for freeing the couple for intimacy. Choosing to make your mate a supreme priority and joining him or her in a permanent relationship lay the foundation for the union of your bodies (one flesh) and the profound connection of your souls (unashamed).

The Importance of Genesis 2:24–25

For the religious aspects of this book, I am relying mostly on what I and other Christians refer to as the Old Testament, though there are several places where I will use the New Testament, particularly for the teachings of Jesus. I tell you this to make a point: the passage from Genesis is the core teaching about marriage in all of the Bible. Not only is it the first major teaching anywhere in Scripture about marriage, but it is repeated by Jesus in his major teaching about marriage.

Jesus spoke of commitment in marriage at a time when the religious teachers who were against him wished to trap him in an argument between those who held more liberal views on divorce and those who advanced more conservative teachings. What Jesus did was to go to this same core passage from Genesis:

> And Pharisees came up to him and tested him by asking, "Is it lawful to divorce one's wife for any cause?" He answered, "Have you not read that he who created them from the beginning made them male and female, and said, 'Therefore a man shall leave his father and his mother and hold fast to his wife, and they shall become one flesh'? So they are no longer two but one flesh. What therefore God has joined together, let not man separate" [Matthew 19:3–6 ESV].

Jesus amplified the Genesis text in several ways. In particular, he emphasized the idea of two becoming one. But he didn't mean that two are meant to become one blob, in which one or both of the people's identities are lost. The idea is that two form a new, highly prized identity of "us" that is to be nurtured and protected. If you were to draw that concept, it might look like this:

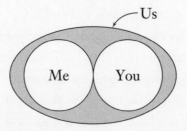

Note that there are three identities implied by the circles: you, me, and us. The boundary that commitment makes around the two creates a third identity of us, and that is the essence of the concept of oneness. In great marriages you will clearly see that this third identity is nurtured, protected, and enjoyed.

In his teaching, Jesus also stressed permanence. His view of commitment overshadowed the religious leaders' concerns about the rules of divorce. In fact, the emphasis on commitment led the disciples to remark that perhaps no one was really up to it! Jesus' disciples objected, "If such is the case of a man with his wife, it is better not to marry" (Matthew 19:10 ESV). Clearly Jesus came down more on the side of the conservative view of divorce; merely being displeased with your wife (men at that time did not contemplate that women could be displeased with their husbands) was not sufficient grounds for ending a marriage. However, he took that view not by appealing to conservative teachings but by appealing to original intent and desire.

Note how quickly even Jesus' disciples became distracted by the calling of commitment rather than the promise of intimacy implied in the idea of oneness and being naked and unashamed. The benefits of true commitment are perhaps obscure to us at times—but they are surely there.

To be totally clear, here is the most important point to take from this discussion: only in the *safety* of a secure commitment is it reasonable to be naked and unashamed. If your heart deeply desires the connection, your mind needs to live out the commitment.

Freedom or Loss of Freedom?

Perhaps the central dilemma of commitment is that it appears to require that you give up some freedom. After all, putting a constraint on your priorities and committing to another for a lifetime does seem like you are losing some freedom. There are two important points not to miss, however.

First, although a kind of loss is involved with commitment because we make the choice to give up or lower the priority of other choices in our lives, commitment results from choice. If you don't make a choice, you are not fully committed. It is the freedom to choose that allows you to become committed to another.

Second, loss of freedom outside the boundaries of the marriage union actually creates new opportunities for a profound level of freedom within them. It protects the kind of safety that is needed to have the best in marriage. So if you feel that joining, or cleaving, implies a loss of freedom, you need to remember that it actually leads to the greater freedom of oneness and openness. If you really want the security and freedom, you have to act out the commitment.

Exercising Your Commitment

Do you act on your commitment? Think about different ways that you show your commitment to your marriage and your mate. Think of ways that your mate shows his or her commitment to you. Then think about other things you could do to show and strengthen your commitment. Pay particular attention to ways you can act that are most meaningful to your mate.

Let me illustrate that point with a story of my own. Near Colorado Springs there is a very high bridge over a canyon called the Royal Gorge. I forget how high the bridge is, but it's a long way down. In fact, it's far enough down that you look carefully at the bridge and its moorings before you walk across it. The last time I walked across that bridge, I first checked to be sure that the ends were securely attached.

What does this have to do with commitment? My point is this: if I didn't think the bridge was very secure, I never would have started across it. Likewise in marriage: when you sense that your commitment is firm, you gain the confidence to venture out. If it's not secure or you're not sure, you will not relax to enjoy the view. In fact, you may not go across the bridge at all.

A Most Wonderful Thing

I believe that it is possible for people to reject themselves—who they are, how they are, what they are. This can be as painful as when others reject them, perhaps even more so. For any number of reasons, some people reject themselves deeply, or at best are quite insecure about who they are. Sometimes, though by no means always, that comes from not being consistently accepted by their parents or other adults when they were children.

Although I think rejection, by oneself and others, can be painful and difficult, I do not think that acceptance of oneself by oneself can ever really make up for a lack of acceptance from those who raised you or with whom you were in prior, serious relationships. We are built for relationship, and in marriage like nowhere else, most of us deeply desire deeper acceptance and full support. In part, this means that one of the greatest potentials of marriage is for you affirm each other through the power of your commitment.

The author Frank Pittman and I once shared a keynote address time slot at the Smart Marriages Conference (in 2002). I gave a talk entitled "What Is It with Men and Commitment, Anyway?" and he followed with a talk entitled "Teaching Men Marriage."[3] I can still remember how he made the point that marriage has such great potential for healing us because of the power of the commitment in it. Among the many things he said, he noted that "People without models and examples of marriage do not know its magical healing power." People who do not have or do not develop a model of commitment in marriage to live by will be deprived of this most special, healing relationship in life.

So here's the point. You cannot be perfect and neither can your mate, but the totality of your acceptance and commitment teaches each other, day by day, that this is okay. Sure, improve yourself and, at times, push your mate to do likewise. But the real power of marriage is in the ongoing, and growing, acceptance of one another that is founded in commitment. One way you can enhance the power of your role as an agent of deep acceptance and healing in the life of your mate (which also, by the way, makes it more likely he or she can do this for you) can be framed in the ancient practice of the Hebrews of conveying a blessing to loved ones.

In Jewish culture as I understand it, from the days of the Patriarchs forward, there has been a powerful tradition of bestowing blessings on loved ones. We most often think about this as something parents do for their children. But this type of blessing is not merely saying "Peace" as your child leaves your home in the morning. It is something much more profound given on special occasions. Gary Smalley and John Trent's excellent book *The Blessing* also describes various specific ways to enact a beautiful giving from one to another.[4] But how does all this relate to commitment?

Although I have focused elsewhere on the fall that is the subject of chapter 3 in Genesis,[5] I'm trying to point out here that the universal elements of commitment that are reflected in the core teaching of Genesis 2:24 make way for the sublime level of connection and acceptance in Genesis 2:25. The fall and its aftermath show the complications that sin and selfishness bring to marriage, and the fundamental way they create barriers (fig leaves, if you will) between husband and wife—barriers that reflect the fact that the perfect safety of "naked and unashamed" has been altered and made more difficult. So the fall accentuates the following point.

Where there can be rejection of one person by another, there can also be acceptance.[6] Where no rejection is possible there can be no acceptance. Commitment in marriage provides the most visible emblem of ongoing acceptance imaginable. Now, I'm not naïve enough to think that all marriages contain a wonderful level of acceptance, but commitment will at least provide a platform for deeper acceptance over time. Marriage is a lifetime message between mates that communicates "I see you" and "I love and accept you." Who else sees more of who you are and what you are like than your mate? Who has any more powerful ability to convey the rich blessing of ongoing commitment and acceptance, despite seeing all your imperfections? Although the great blessings of marriage are not guaranteed, they will surely not happen over time without commitment.

Security in Marriage: An Outmoded Idea?

Is the view of marital commitment portrayed in the previous section still practical today? Can one man and one woman be joined together for life? Is it really possible? Increasingly, you hear "experts" suggest that it is not. Considering that we're living longer than ever, who could stay devoted to the same person for fifty years or more?

If that's your view, please consider one point before you choose to side with the skepticism of our day: aren't the core themes reflected in what is written about Adam and Eve the very desires that most people deeply hope for on their wedding day? Couples want security and safety; they want to be naked and unashamed.

The problem is not the vision; it's the fact that the vision is hard to attain.

Even if you are a skeptic who believes that lifelong commitment is not possible, you can still learn many powerful strategies in this book—ways to act on commitment that can make your marriage stronger. However, I believe that commitment for life is the more powerful and higher view of marriage. If you live out the strategies described here, you will develop a full, and fulfilling, level of commitment in your marriage. Remember that it is the highest view of commitment over the long haul that makes for the most wonderful marriages because of the security that goes with this way of thinking.

Just one caveat: try not to let the higher view of marriage generate unrealistic expectations. Many people have trouble in their marriages because their expectations are unrealistic. For example, some expect that their mate will be able to fulfill *all* their deepest longings and needs. Having such an expectation puts an undue burden on your marriage and increases the likelihood that you will be unhappy. So lowering truly unrealistic expectations is a good thing to do.

When it comes to commitment, however, lowering the bar is not a good idea. A lower view is not consistent with what you want in the deeper regions of your soul. So it's important to keep expectations for commitment high. It *is* realistic to live an "until death do us part" marriage, cherishing and nurturing your relationship for years to come. Such an expectation is only realistic, though, when your dream is fueled by the choices and acts of commitment that produce it. That's what the rest of this book is all about.

KEY COMMITMENT ACTIONS

- Think more about the story of Adam and Eve. Then think about what the expression "naked and not ashamed" means to you.
- Choose to make your family and marriage a priority in your life. What changes do *you* need to make in the way you live?
- Think about what you expect of your marriage and resolve to let go of any unrealistic expectations.

Now add and take your own action steps to strengthen your commitment even more:

_____

_____

_____

STEP TWO

Battling the Myths That Undermine Commitment

Character is that which reveals moral purpose,
exposing the class of things a man chooses or avoids.
ARISTOTLE

Goal of Step Two: The goal of this step is to help you understand and battle within yourself against major myths that undermine a fulfilling and rewarding commitment in marriage.

Chapter 3

Maybe I Can Have It All

A number of years ago, my wife Nancy and I were in the market for a new car. We had two very old Toyotas that we had bought during our graduate school days, and we were finally in a position to do more than just dream about owning a new car. As we investigated every option, our choices narrowed to a Ford Taurus and a Honda Accord. The cost was similar for both, and both cars had good safety records, so we focused on other factors. The Honda was the smaller of the two. We preferred the greater room of the Taurus. But we thought the Honda might be more reliable. After a bit of agonizing, we bought the Taurus.

We made a choice. We had enough money for only one car, so we could not have bought both. The choice of one precluded having the other.

The same concept holds true in every major commitment, especially commitment in marriage. When you commit to following one path, you often have to give up another. And that can be difficult. Many people, after making important decisions, experience "buyer's remorse." They wonder, *What if I made the wrong choice?* As I discussed in the first chapter, we live in a culture in which more and more people resist making the commitment in the first place, living continually in *maybe* land and ending up being the wind watchers I also talked about in Chapter One—people who never bring in a full crop of blessings.

Here's another, more emotional example of having to make a difficult decision. Not long ago I met a couple in their late forties who had no children. All through their late twenties and into their thirties, Jane and Kelly had tried and tried to have a baby. As many of you can understand, they went through years of infertility heartbreak. They tried this doctor and that doctor. They tried most of the high-tech procedures. They prayed. Their friends prayed. But still, there was no baby.

Finally, after ten years of trying everything, they decided they had better think about adopting. They got excited about it and took steps to adopt a baby. Sadly for them, this process turned out to be just as wrenching as the infertility treatment process had been. On two different occasions they were within days of receiving a baby, but in one case the birth mother decided to keep the baby, and in the other a relative of the baby objected to the adoption and initiated legal proceedings, which caused Jane and Kelly to move on.

Finally, at forty-six and forty-seven, Jane and Kelly decided to give up their plans to have a child. It was a very painful decision, but it had become too hard for them to go on, and they felt they were getting too old to start being parents. Of course many couples do begin families at later ages these days, but Jane and Kelly decided that this was not for them.

Their decision, though they were certain it was wise, affected them deeply. Sometimes they wondered, *What if . . . ?* Sometimes they replayed all the factors that had gone into their decision, which was, of course, painful for them. They constantly thought *maybe* we should have done this, or *maybe* we should have done that, or *maybe* we should look into yet another option.

It is agonizing to live on the edge of a major decision. Commitment implies gaining from what you choose but also losing in what you give up (see Chapter Nine). Jane and Kelly decided to turn the corner. They made a mutual commitment to close the door on the dream of having a child and move on. They had other dreams, and there was much to fulfill them ahead. Living in a state of indecision only caused them to miss out on the wonderful things they had.

Some people fail to recognize that commitment means making hard choices among alternatives. Many people do not want to give up one option in order to have another, though they will have neither if they do not make a choice. But choices and priorities are intertwined with commitment.

Making the Choice to Give Up Other Choices

For most people, marriage means choosing to be the lifelong partner of one mate. It's certainly what most people want when they get married, even if they have an otherwise immature understanding of commitment. When you decide to marry, you are choosing one person among many to *stick* with through thick and thin. You are choosing to give up all other possible partners—in the words of the marriage vow, "forsaking all others." Hence, *commitment involves making the choice to give up some choices.* Keeping commitments requires that you recognize the need to give up some other paths.

But giving up other paths runs counter to what is valued and praised in our culture. Our culture values choice or, rather, having choices. "Keep all your options open," people say. Don't give up anything. Recently I noted an advertisement for a book club that read, "Four books, four bucks, and absolutely, positively no commitment!" You get something, and you don't have to give up anything—perfect!

I might sign up for a book club that makes a promise like that. The problem comes when you expect major commitments in life, such as marriage, to come with the same promise. You expect to get something without having to give something else up. This will not happen.

Exercising Your Commitment

Please answer each question here by indicating how strongly you agree or disagree with the idea expressed. Circle the appropriate number between 1 and 5, using the following scale:

> 1 = Strongly disagree;
> 3 = Neither agree nor disagree;
> 5 = Strongly agree.

1. 1 2 3 4 5   I believe that you can make commitments without giving up any options.
2. 1 2 3 4 5   I will give up some things in life in order to have other things that I want more.
3. 1 2 3 4 5   I would rather keep all my options open than make a commitment that requires giving up some choices in the future.

4. 1 2 3 4 5   When I make a commitment to one path, there are usually other paths that must be forsaken.

5. 1 2 3 4 5   Life requires you to make choices, and in making these choices you have to give up some options.

6. 1 2 3 4 5   I won't give up any options unless it's absolutely necessary.

7. 1 2 3 4 5   If you do not ever give things up, there are many other things that you cannot gain.

8. 1 2 3 4 5   So far in life, I have not had to give up options because of choices I have made.

Now, total up your answers to questions 1, 3, 6, and 8.
Next, total up your answers to questions 2, 4, 5, and 7.

If your total for 1, 3, 6, and 8 is greater than your total for 2, 4, 5, and 7, I encourage you to think especially hard about the message of this chapter and whether your beliefs about hanging on to options could get in your way.

Not Having It All Gives You More Freedom

Most of us can probably think of something we currently lack, but we may also think that eventually we can have it. Having it all is a fundamental promise (even a premise) of our culture. Are there limits? Of course there are, but knowing that and living as if you believe it are two different things. It's a dilemma as old as the temptation in the garden.

In the book of Genesis, you can read that God had made a perfect garden for a perfect couple in a relationship designed for total commitment and connection. Adam and Eve had many choices open to them—the whole garden, to be exact—and God told them that they could choose fruit from any tree except one. Almost all of the garden was open to them. Then the serpent tempted Eve and Adam, and got them to focus on the very choice that was off-limits: the fruit of the tree of knowledge of good and evil. Even though Adam and Eve had many choices, they most wanted to make the one choice that was off-limits—forbidden fruit. And having free will, they made that choice.

Like Eve and Adam, we live out this ancient conflict all the time. Most of us really do not want to be told by anyone that we can't make any choice we please. Am I wrong? But such resistance to limits runs counter to the concept of commitment.

Notice the swap Adam and Eve made. *They were offered the mystery of oneness but they freely chose the limits of something that appeared limitless instead.* In reality, that "freedom" led to greater limits, but Adam and Eve were deceived and not able to see that. And that deception lives on. A voice inside most of us continues to say, "You can have the most fulfilling life by keeping all your options open and not giving up a thing." Do you hear that voice in your life? *The paradox is that you can experience more freedom when you accept the limits of commitment.*

My sons love to play in our backyard, for good reason. Within the nice fence that encloses it, they have many choices open to them for playful enjoyment. They are free to swing, spray plants (and each other) with the hose, roll in the grass, run, jump, dig in the dirt, throw a ball, and fiercely battle imaginary warriors. Outside the fence there are dangers: big dogs, bigger kids who might not be careful or kind, fast cars, and so forth. The fence both protects them and gives them the freedom to fully relax and explore what's in bounds.

In all aspects of life, you can accept the many possibilities within a fenced area, or you can jump the fence so you're not denied any options. Jumping the fence is not the path of commitment. Neither is forever sitting on the fence, obsessing about all the *maybes* of life. A mature understanding of commitment includes accepting that some options must be forsaken and some fences will be built. In marriage, the fences that go up around the relationship because of commitment allow barriers within the relationship to be pulled down. A "maybe I do" commitment does not result in the great blessings of marriage. You must decide to be fully in, or you might as well be fully out.

Taking *Maybe* off the Table

As you've read, real commitment requires taking some choices off the table. Sometimes this reality is painful to accept, especially when people are very unhappy in their marriages. The pain, in fact, can lead people to convince themselves that they didn't make their initial commitment freely. "*Maybe* we really didn't mean it. *Maybe* it was not meant to be." Then they rebel against the commitment they willingly expressed on their wedding day.

When you choose a mate, you're saying you're going to "dance with the one that brung ya." Did anyone really hold a gun to your head when you married? Too many married people talk as if that were the case. But I understand the feeling. It's a fairly normal response to intense unhappiness. But it is most often the result of a distortion of the past based on the pain of the present. It's most often caused by rewriting history, not by remembering it clearly and honestly.

There *are* some arranged marriages in the world. At times, shotgun weddings have occurred. For most couples, however, it's not that they were forced into their commitment. Rather, it's that they feel stuck by the commitment they made. Please don't get me wrong.

If you find yourself in such a place, I'm not saying, "You made your bed, now sleep in it." I'll give you many suggestions for actively making your marriage all it can be. But we humans have a tendency not to want to give up choices and sometimes not to want to take responsibility for choices we already made. In Genesis 3, Adam blamed Eve, and Eve blamed the serpent. "It wasn't me who made that choice!" We always want the options, but we don't always want to accept the consequences.

If your marriage is painful, I don't want to imply that it's easy to cope with the reality. Following through on your commitments is often very hard and not much fun. There are blessings to sticking, but it can feel a lot like being stuck at times. Sometimes you may also feel a sense of loss or grief as well. (We'll talk more about loss and grief in Chapter Nine.)

Finding Contentment

Once there was a man who had everything the material life could offer. He had it all, and he explored it all. There were few fences in his life and numerous choices. In the world of my sons' experience, you could say he had one really major backyard to play in. Here is his description of what he had and what he did:

> I made great works. I built houses and planted vineyards for myself. I made myself gardens and parks, and planted in them all kinds of fruit trees. I made myself pools from which to water the forest of growing trees. I bought male and female slaves, and had slaves who were born in my house. I had also great possessions of herds and flocks, more than any who had been before me in Jerusalem. I also gathered for myself silver and gold and the treasure of kings and provinces. I got singers, both

men and women, and many concubines, the delight of the children of man.

So I became great and surpassed all who were before me in
Jerusalem. Also my wisdom remained with me. And whatever
my eyes desired I did not keep from them. I kept my heart from
no pleasure, for my heart found pleasure in all my toil, and this
was my reward for all my toil. Then I considered all that my
hands had done and the toil I had expended in doing it, and
behold, all was vanity and a striving after wind, and there was
nothing to be gained under the sun.

So I turned to consider wisdom and madness and folly. For
what can the man do who comes after the king? Only what has
already been done [Ecclesiastes 2:4–12 ESV].

That passage was written by Solomon. No king was greater in
his time. He had it all in terms of what the world had to offer. Was
he a happy man? Certainly not when he wrote the Book of Ecclesiastes, as was apparent in his journal: "What has a man from all the
toil and striving of heart with which he toils beneath the sun? For
all his days are full of sorrow, and his work is a vexation. Even in
the night his heart does not rest. This also is vanity" (Ecclesiastes
2:22–23 ESV).

How could someone have so much and not be completely happy?
And not only was he not all that happy, he was stressed out. Solomon
also wrote, "Better is a handful of quietness than two hands full of
toil and a striving after wind" (Ecclesiastes 4:6 ESV). We were not
built to be able to hang on to everything and live well.

I read Ecclesiastes often, and I can't help thinking that it is the
chronicle of Solomon's midlife crisis. What are midlife crises, anyway?
Do such things really exist? I think they do for many people, but
they are experienced differently.

I think a midlife crisis is about coming to the full realization that your earthly life is not going to go on forever and that your options in the remaining years are limited by the choices you have already made. The future reality of death is a factor, but I don't think it's the driving force. It's the realization of your limits that pushes the angst. The fact is that you are not going to get to do everything you wish you could do. You are not going to get to do everything you are capable of doing. You may come close, but you're still not going to come as close to having it all as Solomon—and not even he had peace at the height of his glory. Real contentment does not lie on that path.

Have you dealt with a midlife crisis? Are you going through one now? If you are, make it result in a wisely considered midcourse correction.

Commitment Opens the Door to Intimacy

Commitment and the emphasis our culture places on choice are often in fundamental conflict. You cannot commit to one thing or one person while keeping all your options open. Commitment goes against the grain of our culture because it comes with limits.

However, some limits in marriage actually open the door to the deeper meaning in life. More specifically, the limits defined by commitment provide the opportunity for a deeper relationship in marriage. For example, research shows that when partners are more dedicated in their marriage, there is more self-disclosure.[1] That's because commitment in the form of dedication provides a fundamental framework for safety and trust, which promotes closeness and openness.

Veronica and Tom have been married thirty-two years. They have two children, who are now in college. Like any couple, they've had their ups and downs, but they are devoted to each other. They know they are there for each other, support each other, and can be counted on to keep their marriage a priority. With such commitment, both feel little risk in sharing deeply with the other, so they do. They know each other in very intimate ways. They are best friends because their dedication fosters trust. Far from limiting them, their commitment is freeing. This kind of active commitment is the foundation for many years together as friends.

Hence, commitment in marriage—really sticking together, with full dedication—makes it possible to reach the greatest depths of openness. *Naked and unashamed doesn't result from* maybe, *but from* I do *and* I will. Commitment gives you the security to risk greater levels of connection. It doesn't guarantee that you will achieve those levels, but *not* committing virtually assures you that you won't. You can hang on to everything and end up with nothing, or you can commit to your spouse and have a very deep relationship. It's your choice.

I do recognize, by the way, that some people fully commit but their spouse does not, so they don't receive the deeper rewards they should. For most couples, however, partners tend to respond to the other partner's dedication with increased dedication of their own.

Trading Relationships for Things

In today's society, people are too willing to sacrifice important things, such as relationships, for what does not matter nearly so much. To many people, having it all includes having the material goods or notoriety they desire. Don't get me wrong. I'm not railing against a reasonable perspective on material needs or against capitalism. However, many people value *things and forms of success over better relationships with others*, including the ones they love most.

But in her book *You Paid How Much for That?!* (coauthored with William Bailey, Howard Markman, and me), Natalie Jenkins pulls together research that shows how little money has to do with happiness once you get beyond a certain level of financial security. I quote:

> Robert Lane, a professor of political science at Yale University, published a book titled *The Loss of Happiness in Market Democracies.* In that book, he showed how studies document an overall decline in the number of people who regard themselves as happy in the United States, which is one of the richest countries in the world. He concluded that, except for the very poor, larger incomes have almost no effect on happiness.
>
> As we said, various studies of the connection between money and happiness have come up with conflicting results. We make sense of the data this way. If you are living in poverty, having more money will likely make a huge, positive difference in your life. In contrast, if your core material needs in life are met, having more money might be nice, but it's not likely to make you a lot happier. There are diminishing returns. That's why, even in studies that show that money and happiness are associated, money in and of itself tells you little about happiness once you tease out other variables known to be associated with happiness, such as high self-esteem, security, and healthy family relationships.[2]

So, what does lead to happiness? Robert Lane concludes that the real source of contentment and happiness in economies where most people have their basic needs met is family and friendships—relationships![3] In fact, studies by the National Opinion Research Center show that if you are happy in your marriage, you are quite

? Did You Know . . .

Do the researchers' findings mentioned here mean that there is no relationship among marriage, money, and happiness in life? No. In fact, Linda Waite and Maggie Gallagher, in their review of research in their book *The Case for Marriage*, note that those who are most likely to be both happy in life and also financially well off later in life are those who succeed in commitment in marriage.[5] Money can't buy you love, but love lived in commitment can provide a better financial future for both you and your mate.

likely to be happy, overall, in life.[4] Yet if you are not happy in your marriage, the odds of your being happy in life are nil.

So where do you want to put your greater energies? Into having more and more money, or into your marriage (while doing enough to provide the money you need to live responsibly and well)? Both are important, but putting your marriage first is most crucial in life.

Here's a story about a couple who seem to have it all: money, cars, a nice house, three wonderful kids, and satisfying jobs. Jennifer and Mike have bought all the latest toys, they're up on the latest social and political issues, and they're connected to the right people. They are pillars of their church and the PTA. Both exercise a minimum of four hours a week. He is a partner in an accounting firm, and she is a real estate agent.

They're an impressive couple—but they have empty lives. They are rich in things and impoverished in relationships, including their marriage and the relationships they have with their children. They have little time together and not a lot with their children. Sure, their children are involved in all the coolest activities—they need planning calendars as much as Jennifer and Mike do. But the times when their lives overlap are minimal. Jennifer sometimes wonders which they have more of: a family or a business. They seem to have it all, but what do they really have?

One of the most negative consequences of keeping all your options open is that you may end up with nothing, especially as far as your relationships go. Do you know the story about the monkey who wants to eat all the food in a jar? He likes the food so much that he grabs such a big handful of it that he can't get his fist out of the jar. The only way he can get some food out is if he grabs less of it—and learns that less is more.

Here's an irony for you. Today, in our society, we have more freedom to engage in deeper relationships than most people have ever had throughout history. We have more leisure time, or at least the possibility of it. Many of us can maintain a good standard of living. But by always trying to have more things, people often sacrifice time they should be spending on relationships. *They trade relationships for stuff.* How many couples, for instance, buy houses at the very limit of what they can qualify for? Then they have to work more and more to make ends meet, further reducing time together and time to be with their family.

Solomon pegged the driving force behind how hard many of us work: "Then I saw that all toil and all skill in work come from a man's envy of his neighbor. This also is vanity and a striving after wind" (Ecclesiastes 4:4 ESV).

Do you envy certain people? Would you like to have what they have? Would you like to do better than they are doing? If you experience envy, remember Solomon. He had it all and did it all. No one beat him in his day. Many people must have envied him. But he concluded that trying to have it all was meaningless, a "chasing after the wind." You can never feed this beast enough to satisfy it. Being driven by envy or trying to have every material good does not lead to a life of meaning.

Having Everything and Nothing

In chapter 4 of Ecclesiastes, Solomon wrote,

> Again, I saw vanity under the sun: one person who has no other, either son or brother, yet there is no end to all his toil, and his eyes are never satisfied with riches, so that he never asks, "For whom am I toiling and depriving myself of pleasure?" This also is vanity and an unhappy business [Ecclesiastes 4:7–8 ESV].

Solomon wrote those words without reference to a specific person, but I think he was writing about himself. He was a man with everything, with all his options open, with the ability to explore all his choices. But as various translations say, he was all alone. He had an empty life and was therefore not content. He didn't have true riches.

In the following passage, Solomon described someone who was a tireless worker, who had gained much success and had a lot to show for it—a lot of stuff. But where did his choices—his commitments— lead him? In contrast to the sad words about the empty life of the man who "had it all," Solomon wrote some of the most sublime words ever written about the joy of being in a relationship:

> Two are better than one, because they have a good reward for their toil. For if they fall, one will lift up his fellow. But woe to

him who is alone when he falls and has not another to lift him up! Again, if two lie together, they keep warm, but how can one keep warm alone? And though a man might prevail against one who is alone, two will withstand him—a threefold cord is not quickly broken [Ecclesiastes 4:9–12 ESV].

These lines are so beautiful that they are often incorporated into wedding ceremonies. On the day I married Nancy, our pastor added a vow to the ceremony that we had not talked about beforehand. He asked me to promise to keep Nancy warm. Of all the things that were said and done that day, those were the words that stood out most to me and to Nancy and my mother. Promising to keep Nancy warm encompasses so much. It's a powerful promise with far more potential for contentment than material goods can offer.

I know it's fashionable in some places to be committed to material goods at the expense of relationships. It's almost trendy. That does not diminish the fact that the situation is a very real dilemma for most of us. We can work harder to chase after the wind and try to have it all, or we can cut back, pace ourselves, accept less on some fronts, and have more on the home front. These choices are not simple, especially in a culture that will not reward us for choosing the latter. Material success and wealth are glorified every day, all day, across our country. Examples of healthy, thriving marital relationships are not held up for us to see.

If you are in the throes of the relationship-versus-things conflict and are choosing marriage and family, expect a fight—a fight with the values of our culture and, much more troubling, with yourself about what you value most in your life. The fight may be hard and painful. But you will be making the right choice.

Choosing Commitment When You Have Fewer Options

There are certainly many couples who want to have it all, but there are also many couples worried about losing it all. These are people who are so on the edge financially that thinking about cutting back on work demands or reprioritizing to favor family time is not within the realm of possibility. If they cut back on work they may not be able to feed their family or might end up being dependent on the government.

If you are in this boat, you probably don't have some of the options we talk about in this book. However, even if your choices are more limited to begin with, you still have some choice about how you act on your commitments. Within the scope of your life's reality, you can carve out space for your marriage and your children. Although it may be much harder for you, it's still the right thing to do.

To those of you with greater resources and options, I encourage you to think about how you can help families with greater burdens. In Ecclesiastes 4, which addresses ambition and priorities, Solomon deals directly with the topic of oppression. When family members are doing all they can to support themselves, but the parents still cannot steal time for each other or their children, they are being oppressed by their circumstances, and maybe by the culture in which they live. Give this some thought. I'm not arguing for a governmental solution, though the government can provide much-needed support for families who are struggling beyond the edge. I am suggesting that we all look for opportunities to help others. In fact, that could be one way you and your mate draw together more deeply in life.

We are built for more than realizing our material dreams. We will be deeply satisfied in life when we are able to experience the wonder of a warm and secure relationship with a mate.

 KEY COMMITMENT ACTIONS

- Discuss with your mate the idea that commitment means taking some choices off the table. Talk about the fact that when you married you resolved to "forsake all others."
- Think about a time when you gave up something important to you, and your sacrifice resulted in something beneficial to your mate or your marriage. Resolve to do at least one thing like that again soon and to keep up the pattern.
- Do something special this week that shows your spouse that she or he is your priority.

Now add and take your own action steps to strengthen your commitment even more:

_____

_____

_____

STEP TWO

Chapter 4

Maybe You Can Wait

George MacDonald was a great influence on author C. S. Lewis. He too was an author, as well as a poet known for deeply moving pieces with strong spiritual overtones; he was born in 1824 and lived until 1905. The verses that follow here are from his poem "Willie's Question," and I've chosen them because they're a conversation between a father and a son about what is most important in life and how to be great.

> Willie speaks:
> *Is it wrong, the wish to be great,*
> *For I do wish it so?*
> *I have asked already my sister Kate;*
> *She says she does not know. . . .*

This morning a trumpet blast
Made all the cottage quake;
It came so sudden and shook so fast
It blew me wide awake.
It told me I must make haste,
And some great glory win,
For every day was running to waste,
And at once I must begin. . . .

The father answers:
The harder you run that race,
The farther you tread that track,
The greatness you fancy before your face
Is the farther behind your back. . . .

Be admiral, poet, or king,
Let praises fill both your ears,
Your soul will be but a windmill thing
Blown round by its hopes and fears. . . .

The father speaks:
Think: is there nothing, great or small,
You ought to go and do?

Willie answers:
Let me think—I ought to feed
My rabbits, I went away
In such a hurry this morning! Indeed,
They've not had enough today!

The father speaks:
That is his whisper low!
That is his very word!

You had only to stop and listen, and so
Very plainly you heard! . . .

Willie speaks:
But that's so easily done!
It's such a trifling affair!
So nearly over as soon as begun,
For that he can hardly care!

The father answers:
You are turning from his call
If you let that duty wait;
You would not think any duty small
If you yourself were great.[1]

The son, Willie, desires desperately to be great, but his ideas for greatness involve being great in the eyes of others. However, he learns that greatness comes from fulfilling duties to loved ones—in this case, his pet rabbit.

What interferes with your ability to make your mate the priority in your life? Fame and fortune, as Willie desires? Pleasures and hobbies pursued to the exclusion of time with your love? This chapter is about priorities and how hard it can be to act on what we say they are. As Willie's father tries to teach him, we'll see how greatness comes from doing small things, such as following through and meeting the needs of the ones you love.

Your priorities are the things that are most important to you, and having the right priorities is crucial to your marriage. Making the right choices among all the competing demands for your time will help you live out your devotion to your mate. Making the wrong choices may cause you to get mired on the side of the road you wish to travel.

In my research on marital commitment, I've found that making one's mate and marriage a high priority is a key part of dedication.[2] No surprise there, right? It's a simple, logical concept, but living out that concept is not so simple. The fact is, even when you are fully dedicated to your mate, there are so many appealing options available that you can let slide the one focused on marriage and family. Options test our priorities on a daily basis. And when push comes to shove, when we're in a crunch, our priorities can get lost.

As I said in the previous chapter, commitment is about making the choice to give up other choices. It's important to recognize that this is something called for continually in marriage, not simply something symbolized on the wedding day. Like Willie's rabbit, priorities are often reflected in the small things, the small decisions, and the small needs of loved ones—not always, and maybe not often, in grand and momentous decisions.

Keeping marriage a high priority is not a comfortable topic for most of us, because we all experience pressures and pulls in life that tempt us to put our marriage on the back burner. Sometimes you might like to light a fire under your mate's behind in that regard— but I encourage you to light one under your own first! All of us feel the tension between our priorities and how we actually act—I'd even go so far as to suggest that you are not normal if you don't feel that tension at least occasionally. But if your priorities don't hold fast most of the time, your relationship will go downhill.

Before we go on to things you can do to keep your marriage a high priority in your life, I have one cautionary note. Much of what you'll read in this chapter will challenge you and might make you feel guilty. Please don't get stuck in unproductive guilt. If you need to make some changes, guilt can be a fine impetus to do so. But don't feel so bad that you get stuck in a ditch. If you feel guilt after reading this chapter but nothing comes from it, then both of us will have failed—you in a crucial task in life and I in my hope of encouraging you to live according to your priorities. If you are having a significant problem with priorities in your life, don't feel guilty; makes some changes.

"No-ing" Rather Than Knowing

Rick and Margo met when he was twenty-seven and she was twenty-five. They worked for the same software firm, he in development and she in sales. She was very drawn to his intelligence and drive. She could see that he was going places in the firm. He was very drawn to her outgoing personality, her way of approaching issues in life, her humor, and how comfortable he felt talking to her. While they dated, he made plenty of time to see her, even though the projects he was working on demanded tremendous amounts of time and energy. They married after a year.

Ten years and two kids later, Rick was indeed the star of the software development team. But Margo never saw him. His work required long hours, he had frequent deadlines, and pressure from the company's highest levels never let up. He came home later every night, rarely before eight. Years earlier Margo had cut back to working part time for the software company to spend more time with their children, but she felt as though she was raising them herself. She was frazzled. This wasn't the vision she had had for her life with Rick.

Occasionally Margo confronted Rick about his absences. Each time, he did a compelling job of convincing her that she and the kids were his real priorities. She wanted to believe him, but she couldn't see how it could be true. When she asked him if he could attend their older child's school program, he answered, "No honey, sorry. I have to finish my project, or I'll be in a real fix." When she asked him to sit down and talk with her before they went to sleep, he said, "No, I can't tonight. I'd love to, but I have this crucial presentation in the morning." What amazed her most was his response when she asked him if he wanted to "get close tonight"—which was their way of saying "make love." He said, "No, I really can't. I'm so wiped out I have to get some sleep." *He was "no-ing" her but not knowing her.*

Margo understood the pressure Rick was under, but she had married him to have a life with him, and he had married her to have a life with her—that's what they both had wanted when they had said "I do." Margo was very disappointed, as was Rick, though to a lesser degree. Although he knew that the conflicts between them were no simple matter, he truly thought (and he was correct) that if he gave any less of himself to his work he would lose his job. Many others had. He felt trapped in a work situation in which the expectations and the pace were brutal. But slowing down would require him and Margo to rethink their entire lifestyle.

Why do we put our mate last on our priority list? If you do, like Rick, consider this for a moment: it may be because your mate is committed to you for life. If you believe that he or she will be there for you, then you don't have to pay as much attention as you do to others who actually don't matter nearly as much in the long run.

When you act in this way, you're making a big presumption. You are presuming that your mate can take all sorts of neglect. But presuming on your commitment to your spouse will erode the quality of your relationship over time. That's because, after having promised to love and cherish your spouse, you say, in essence, "You can and will wait; *this* can't." In other words, the very commitment you have each made to the other makes it easy, at times, to make one another wait because something else is—or seems—more urgent. At times, that is a very reasonable way to think. In fact, it truly is one of the blessings of commitment, because it allows each of you to do what you need to do in other areas of life and still count on your mate being there for you. But when the "no-ing" is chronic and it interferes with knowing each other, you need to do some serious reevaluating.

The Problem with "Yes"

Before my son Luke turned six, he uttered the most profound words I have heard. His words get to the root of how our priorities are rooted in who we say no to and who we say yes to in life. Of my two boys, Luke is the one who came tuned from the factory to use the word *no*. From his earliest days of talking, "no" has been a word that comes easily to his little lips. This is especially the case when he is asked to stop doing something he is enjoying and to start doing something that needs to be done, as demonstrated in these conversations:

> DAD: Luke, you need to go brush your teeth—now.
>
> LUKE: No.
>
> DAD: Luke, time for bed. Hop to it.
>
> LUKE: No.
>
> DAD: Luke, how about if we go and throw the football? You haven't been outside all day.
>
> LUKE: No.
>
> DAD: Luke, do you want some ice cream?
>
> LUKE: No . . . um, wait. Sure.

You get the idea. One day, I asked him to stop playing with something and get ready for dinner. Surprise, he said, no. But I was in a pretty good mood and felt like kidding around some.

> DAD: Luke, let me hear you say yes. You can do it. It sounds like this: yeesssss.
>
> LUKE: *(giggling)* No.
>
> DAD: *(playfully)* Oh, come on, you can do it. Let me hear you say yes.
>
> LUKE: No.
>
> DAD: You are such a "no" boy; let's try being a "yes" boy. It would be fun!
>
> LUKE: *(laughing)* No.
>
> DAD: Yes, yes, yes!
>
> LUKE: *(on the ground in hysterics)* No, no, no!
>
> DAD: *(not looking for anything serious here)* Luke, how come you say no all the time?
>
> LUKE: Because yes takes too much time.

Have you ever had one of those moments when your child (if you have a child) says something so profound that it takes you a moment to fully register it? This was one of those moments. I knew Luke had just uttered, in his little almost-six-year-old voice, something amazing.

Let me repeat his phrase and draw attention to it. *Yes takes too much time!*

Luke had just told me the real secret to preserving priorities in life, something that most adults haven't learned: saying no more than saying yes. Luke knows both his mind and his priorities, so when someone asks him to do something that's not on his list, he says no. Now, that doesn't always work out so well for him in life, but he understands that if he says yes to me, it means he's shifting from his priorities to mine.

Maybe you need to say no more often to requests and offers that will compete with what needs to be most important to you in life—your mate and your family. Those are the people to whom you should be saying yes more than anyone else.

Exercising Your Commitment

A key way to look at dedication is to consider what your priorities are. How do you actually live your life, and what does this say about your commitment? The following will help both you and your partner consider your priorities. Answer the questions separately, then compare notes without being defensive.

In column one, list what you consider your top five priorities in life, from greatest to least importance. In column two, list what you think your partner would say are *your* top five priorities. In column three, list what you believe are *your partner's* top five priorities. Some possible priorities for you to consider are listed below the columns. Be as specific as possible with your answers.

Your rating of your priorities	Your guess of your partner's rating of your priorities	Your rating of what you believe are your partner's priorities
1. _____	1. _____	1. _____
2. _____	2. _____	2. _____
3. _____	3. _____	3. _____
4. _____	4. _____	4. _____
5. _____	5. _____	5. _____

Possible Priorities:

Work/career	House/home	Possessions	Friends
Children	Sports	Hobbies	Pets
Your partner	Future goals	Relatives	TV
God and faith	Religion	Education	Coworkers
Car	Environmentalism	Politics	The arts

Intended Versus Actual Priorities

Let's look again at Rick and Margo. When they took a minute to talk about priorities, Rick was reassuring because he really believed what he was saying. He'd say, "Honey, it will all get better later this year when I finish this one major project," and he'd mean it. But a prophet he wasn't. Sure, there were times when things were better than usual, but not often enough. Rick's *intended* priorities were Margo and the kids. The problem was that his *actual* priorities were different. He was aware of the difference and so was she, but he found it so unpleasant to think about that he tried to put it out of his mind. Even though he wanted to be more dedicated to Margo than to his work, he couldn't stand to look too closely at all the evidence that he really didn't live that way. He wanted to stick by her side, but felt stuck because of the pressure of work and the need to perform.

Many people in our fast-paced world struggle every day with the difference between their intended and their actual priorities. Spouses and children can handle the discrepancy for periods of time. They can make allowances. They can understand, in part because of their faith in the future. But when what's on the back burner is rarely stirred or moved to the front, problems develop.

In Rick's case, while he made great money and continued to be a star at work, his marriage became an empty shell. He provided incredibly well financially for his wife and children, but that wasn't very satisfying to either Margo or Rick. If Rick hopes to change so that he acts on his intended priorities more often, he'll have to set apart time for the essential experiences of marital life.

The Sanctification of Everyday Life

Sanctification, consecration, and *holy* are words generally restricted to religious use. I want to draw on their key meanings in that context but use the basic concepts for thinking about what marriages need. These are different words in English, but they have the same Hebrew and Greek roots and incorporate the concepts of "pure and devoted," "separate," and "set apart for a particular use or purpose, particularly for the purposes of God." They are great words that reflect powerful concepts. Our modern word *dedicated* may come closest to the root meaning of these words. For now, let's think about dedication in terms of "something set apart."

Let me illustrate. Nancy and I have some very fine china that belonged to my maternal grandmother. My mother gave it to us some years ago because she had few occasions to use it. We are grateful to have this china. It's old, beautiful, and very special because it was my grandmother's. But we rarely eat on these dishes. They come out only once a year or so for special occasions.

This china is *dedicated*. It's set aside only for use with certain meals. It's not sanctified in the sense of being devoted to the Lord, but it is set apart for special use. It has been dedicated to a special purpose.

If your life reflects a high degree of dedication to your mate, you live in ways that set apart your relationship. You make time for your mate—and more often than once a year! If it's really dedicated time, you jealously guard it and choose it over your other options and possibilities. Sanctifying your priorities in this nonreligious sense is the secret to living your priorities when you have an abundance of options. Although the competing pressures can be many and varied, you win a small victory whenever you set apart time devoted to your partner. This can be time when you do something *for* your partner or, most important, when you do something *with* your partner.

Putting the Big Rocks First

In his book *First Things First*, Stephen Covey describes a powerful illustration that he and others have used in workshops.[3] Imagine this scene. You are at a time management seminar soaking up tips on how to use your time more effectively. The presenter sets a large jar on the table in the front of the room, placing beside it all sorts of softball-size rocks. He says to the crowd, "How many of these rocks do you think I can fit into this jar?" Someone guesses thirteen. Another guesses nine. Still another guesses twelve. The presenter begins to place the rocks into the jar one at a time, counting as he goes: one, two, three, four, and so forth, asking the group if the jar is full each time he adds a rock. The crowd keeps saying no until the rocks nearly reach the top. Nine, ten, eleven, twelve. That's it. Twelve rocks fit in the jar. The audience agrees that the jar is full.

Next, the presenter brings out a bucket filled with smaller rocks and pours them into the jar. They filter all around the bigger rocks. As the man pours, he asks the audience, "Is it full?" "No!" they roar, because they know what's next. Sand. Then water. Then the jar really looks full.

Finally the presenter says to the group, "What's the point?" As Covey relates the story in his book, a woman raises her hand and says something like this: "The point is that there are many nooks and crannies and spaces of time in life that we are just wasting and not using to the fullest." The presenter considers the point, then says, "Nope, that's not the point." The audience, which has been focused on efficiency and organization, is taken aback a bit. Then the presenter says, "The point is this. If the big rocks don't go in the jar first, they don't get in at all."

It's a profound illustration. It's about setting apart time. You see, the big rocks are the things that you believe are most important in your life. They are your *intended* priorities. But all of us have full jars, no matter what size they are. We have only a certain amount of time—we cannot create more. If your rocks are seldom in the jar and mostly out sitting on the table, then they are not being acted on. They are not your *actual* priorities.

I first read about the rocks-and-jar illustration while on vacation with Nancy and our sons. The boys were tucked away, asleep in bed, and Nancy and I were reading near the crackling fire in the fireplace. It was a nice, quiet setting, good for reflection. I was so captivated by the illustration that I read it to Nancy. She likewise thought it wonderful.

A few days later, we were back in Denver sitting in our living room with the boys playing nearby. The image was still in my mind. I turned to Nancy and said, "Honey, you know you are one of the big rocks." Nancy turned warmly toward me and said, "Yeah, but am I in the jar?" It was one of the many times she's given me targeted, tender feedback about my life. I heard what she said very positively.

The principle of sanctification gets to the heart of the basic tension between various priorities in your life. You act on your marital priorities by setting apart time and space for your mate before everything else crowds them out. What's in your jar? What's left out?

? ? *Did You Know . . .*

There are many ways to help make your intended priorities your actual priorities. Here are a few things you can do to set apart special time in your marriage:

- Make regular dates to take a walk together. Then hold hands and talk about interesting and enjoyable things, not problems. Be together as friends.
- Make it your business to be home at dinnertime so that the entire family can share a meal.
- Schedule a date to have fun with your spouse and agree to make problems and concerns off limits during these special times.
- Make time in your schedule to work on problems and issues with your spouse. Setting apart these moments will keep your marriage on track.

In addition to setting aside special time with your mate now (see the "Did You Know . . ." box), you can also plan time together further in the future. This can be motivational. Anticipating doing something is almost as much fun as really doing it. But your plans don't have to be grand or elaborate to have this effect. What's fun for you and your spouse? What's fun for the whole family to do? Planning for a special time a few days or a few months away can help keep you close. I know many families who have built regular Saturday pizza and movie nights into their schedule so that the whole family can relax together at least once a week. Something as simple as that can help see you and your family through tough days. Sharing fun is an amazingly powerful way to help couples stay bonded and follow their vision.

A friend of mine, Janice Levine (who coedited *Why Do Fools Fall in Love?*), calls shared time with spouse and children "holy" moments. You might think that *holy* is too strong a word for this kind of togetherness and that it should be reserved only for activities devoted to God. But even though my friend is not of the same faith background as I am, I, and I think you, can understand exactly what she means when she uses the word this way.

Someone who learned about the need to spend time acting on priorities was Moses. Moses was a pretty busy fellow. At some point in his life, he penned this verse: "So teach us to number our days that we may get a heart of wisdom" (Psalm 90:12 ESV). With those words he made the profound connection between understanding that our days are numbered and living wisely. That wisdom comes from recognizing limits, in not having the false belief that time and space are limitlessness. If you can number your days, you can accept that they are limited, and if you accept that concept, you can accept the need to prioritize, because there is not enough time to do it all.

We all need to carve out space for the best things. You can't create more time, but you can be more creative in making the most of the time you have.

Managing Ambition

Wrongly directed ambition is another competitor for time that you should be spending with your spouse and children. The story Solomon told of a man who has everything and nothing (which we focused on in Chapter Three) is a vivid example of ambition gone awry. The man achieved a great deal, but he was not content to sit around and enjoy the day-to-day life of kingly pleasures. He went for the gusto. He was ambitious, but blindly ambitious; he was headed nowhere at 190 miles an hour. He had material wealth but no relationships.

Here's the key: ambition of the sort that drove Solomon involved winning out over others, but commitment is about walking *with* others through life. They are not the same.

A true confession here: I am highly motivated to pursue both my ambition as well as my commitment. These two forces wrestle in my soul. To be sure, not all ambition is wrong, and some commitments are unwise. However, wrongly directed ambition has no sincere regard for the needs of people. With it you can justify just about anything, even sacrificing your mate and your children. Ambition whispers in your ear, "They'll wait for you while you go after your goals. They'll understand."

But maybe they will not wait. Maybe they shouldn't have to, even if they would. Commitment reins you in. It asks you, "For whom am I toiling?" It's a good question. What's *your* answer?

KEY COMMITMENT ACTIONS

- Discuss with your partner the importance of setting aside time for one another. Consider if you used to do this more and resolve to increase the time you do spend together.
- Think about your schedule and the different activities and events you're involved in. Decide on at least one thing you usually do that you can say no to in the near future. Maybe this week! Once you say no, spend the newly free time doing something enjoyable with your mate.
- Do at least one of the things suggested in the "Did You Know . . ." box. Try listing some specific ways the two of you could take these kinds of action—and begin planning to do what you listed.

Now add and take your own action steps to strengthen your commitment even more:

_____

_____

_____

STEP TWO

Chapter 5

Maybe the Grass Is Greener

In Chapter Three, I talked about how Nancy and I bought our first new car together many years after graduate school. We looked at the Ford Taurus and the Honda Accord and, after considering size (the Ford was bigger), reliability (the data made us think the Honda would be more reliable), and safety (both were equally highly rated), we chose the Taurus. But just because we chose the Taurus didn't mean that Honda went out of business or that there were no Honda Accords on the road. Just as in that scenario, when we choose to marry we pledge to forsake all others, but that doesn't make all the other people in our world disappear.

Think about cars a bit longer. Once you have picked one, when do you think most about others you might have chosen but didn't? When you are unhappy with the way the one you chose is working

out. Did I think about a Honda when the Ford was running perfectly? No. I thought about it when the Ford needed repairs or
expensive maintenance. (When the Ford's transmission went out,
you can believe I thought, *I bet that Honda wouldn't have broken down
on me like this.*)

My point is that we think most about the Honda when we're
unhappy with the Ford. And we can be unhappy with the Ford if
we have not been taking very good care of it—not polishing it, not
maintaining it, not driving it carefully. We can also be unhappy
because we know all the car's faults; it's much harder to think about
what might not have been great about the car we didn't choose. The
comparison is fundamentally unfair. It's also unfair to compare the
Ford we haven't taken such great care of with a brand-new Honda
we see on the showroom floor.

No matter how good or wise a choice you've made, there will
be times when you aren't completely happy with it. This chapter is
about what to do when a car you might have chosen looks better
than the one you picked—when the grass looks greener. When those
times come around, you need to put your commitment into action.
You need to protect all you have built with your spouse from unfair
comparisons, "what-ifs," and "maybes."

More Than Just Friends

Sometimes, even though you're happily married, a friendship with
someone who is not your spouse can turn into an attraction that can
threaten your marriage. Take, for example, Kirsten and Greg and
Alice and Jack. Both couples had been happily married for several
years, but when Kirsten and Jack started playing on the same co-ed
softball team at the rec center, a bond began to form.

Alice hadn't been interested in playing on the team, and Greg's work schedule interfered. Each felt fine about their mates playing, though, and encouraged them to go and have fun. Jack, however, soon began looking forward to practices and games because he became fond of talking to Kirsten; she seemed to enjoy his company as well. Jack felt a bit concerned about what he was feeling, but he thought, *It's no big deal; we're just having some fun.* Kirsten had some uncomfortable thoughts, too, but neither of them talked about their attraction or the conflict they felt inside.

Instead of understanding that his feelings for Kirsten were a threat to his marriage and taking steps to protect his marriage, Jack started to fantasize about being with Kirsten—not Alice. His fantasies weren't so much sexual as they were about simply enjoying being with Kirsten, talking and sharing good times. Because his thoughts weren't explicitly sexual, Jack had a hard time seeing their danger and that he was becoming more and more attracted to Kirsten. He'd chosen the Ford years ago, but was letting himself be tempted by the Accord right now.

As his attraction grew into an obsession, Jack became more dissatisfied with Alice. Although his feelings for Kirsten hadn't grown out of unhappiness with Alice, he felt more alive with Kirsten and liked the way that felt. He started comparing Alice to Kirsten, and Kirsten always came out on top—more positive, more beautiful, more energetic, more fun to talk with, more in shape, more everything.

All of that made Jack resent Alice. *Why can't she be more like Kirsten?* he asked himself over and over. As he grew more unhappy with Alice, he became distant and defensive when they were together. Their marriage suffered. But because Jack wouldn't talk about what was happening, Alice didn't have a clue about what had changed between them. She only knew they were growing apart—painfully.

Jack eventually became so unhappy with Alice that he decided to leave the marriage. He decided that what he had with Alice just wasn't enough for him. He wanted more. He wanted his true soul mate, he thought, and Alice couldn't be it because no one would ever be this dissatisfied if he were married to his true soul mate. (We'll deal more with this issue in Chapter Seven.) Jack's marriage ended because he hadn't seen the warning signs for what they were and hadn't acted on them. If he had taken steps to follow through on his commitment to Alice and protect their love, things would have ended much differently.

But what happened with Kirsten? Though Jack had hoped she would leave Greg, she did not. Kirsten had noticed the warning signs and taken them seriously. She didn't believe a temporary infatuation meant she'd married the wrong person, but it did cause her to think about how to get back on track with Greg and grow together. Most important of all, she remembered that she had made a choice to give up other options, and remained true to her dedication to Greg.

Jack succumbed to thoughts that *maybe* the grass was greener; when he began to be certain that it was, he allowed such thoughts to destroy his marriage. But Kirsten realized in time that maybe the grass wasn't greener, and even if it was, she wasn't going to jump the fence.

Even when you're very committed to your spouse, you can still experience an attraction to someone else. Men are only slightly more likely than women to think seriously about alternatives; it happens to both men and women.[1] What matters is what you do when that happens. The rest of this chapter provides help and understanding if you have been attracted to someone else, and ways to keep attractive alternatives from destroying your marriage.

Alternative Monitoring

Theorists and researchers use the term *alternative monitoring* for thinking about what it would be like to be with someone other than your mate.[2] Studies show that when people are less dedicated, they spend more time thinking about the alternatives and the other people with whom they might be happier.[3] The following are examples of thoughts that characterize this process:

> *What if I were not with my wife and could be with Maria instead?*
> *What if I left my husband to be with William?*
> *I'd rather be with her than the woman I married.*

When you pick one path, it's natural to wonder about the others, especially if the path you've chosen gets rocky. But thinking seriously about alternatives is a prime indicator of how unhappy you are with your mate. If you are very happy most of the time, you may never have what-if thoughts, but that's not the case for most people. That's why commitment matters so much. It takes you through the tougher times. If you are less dedicated, you'll monitor alternatives more seriously, but if you are more dedicated, you'll protect your marriage even when you are attracted to others.

Maybes and what-ifs are the most dangerous when your commitment to your marriage is lagging and the person you're thinking of is available (that is, single or in the process of divorce).

Cindy and Martin—and Frank

Cindy and Martin had been married for twelve years. They had three children between the ages of five and nine. Like most couples, they'd had their ups and down, but basically their marriage was good.

Then Martin, a salesman, was made a district manager and had to start traveling more. The new work left him tired and less available to the family. This caused Cindy to be stressed and unhappy. And because both she and Martin were busier than ever, they stopped going out together and became increasingly irritable with each other.

During this period Cindy, a pharmacist, began to talk more and more with her coworker Frank. She and Frank, who was attractive and divorced, had been working together for five years and had grown to appreciate each other as friends. As Cindy became more unhappy at home, she became increasingly happy to share her thoughts and feelings at work with Frank. Frank really listened to her and understood the stress she was under.

Cindy soon realized that her attraction to Frank was growing beyond mere friendship. She liked feeling what she felt, but it also scared her. *After all, I'm married to Martin, not to Frank,* she reflected. But Frank seemed very interested in her. She wondered if they would date if she left Martin, and started to play various scenarios over and over in her mind.

Frank was an attractive alternative for Cindy both because she was unhappy at home and because Frank was actually a great guy. She would have found him attractive even if she had not been upset with Martin. Fortunately, Cindy was committed to Martin. She was not all that happy with him at that point in their lives, but she was dedicated to him and their marriage. That made her conflicted about her feelings for Frank—she was uncomfortable about them, but she was not sure what to do about them, either. She wished they would just go away.

The good news is that bells went off in Cindy's head—and she listened to them. She became aware that there was a real threat to her marriage, and the threat was not so much Frank as her attraction to Frank. Let's talk more about that threat before we learn more about Cindy and Martin and Frank.

Did You Know . . .

Through research on infidelity, we've learned that the vast majority of Americans say that spouses should be faithful to each other.[4] This is true for people from all walks of life. But like so many things in life, what people say about fidelity and what they do are often two different things. In large surveys, up to 25 percent of men and 15 percent of women say they have had extramarital sex at least once—and that doesn't count all the people in the surveys who may eventually cheat on a spouse nor all the extramarital encounters that fall short of sex.

Although it's hard to predict who will end up having an affair, on average, people who have had affairs have these characteristics:

- They are less satisfied in their marriages.
- They are less satisfied with their marital sex life.
- They tend to be less religious.
- They tend to hold attitudes regarding infidelity that are more accepting than other people's.

Whether or not a person has these characteristics, it would be unwise for anyone to think he or she was immune. Too often, relationships that start off innocently enough develop into something more serious over time. It is important to be aware of situations that could lead down the slippery slope of temptation. If feelings for someone other than your spouse have already developed, trying to suppress them—trying not to think about them—may backfire, because sometimes that can make the attraction more intense. Research suggests that the most protective strategy is to refocus on your dedication to your spouse and strengthen your commitment to your marriage.

Perceiving the Threat to Commitment

Researchers Dennis Johnson and Caryl Rusbult found that when people are more dedicated, they perceive attractive alternatives as a threat to their relationship.[5] In response to this threat, dedicated people internally devalue the attractiveness of the alternatives to protect their commitment to their partners. In other words, instead of wondering how delightful it might be to be with other people, they look for what might not be so good about the alternatives.

Like Cindy, you have the choice either to dwell on the what-ifs or to put that energy into nurturing your marriage and making it as rich as possible. After laying some theological foundations in the next section, I'll present specific strategies for protecting your marriage from attractive alternatives.

What About the Big Ten?

This is a section in which I'm going to let my religious side show pretty clearly. So if you are a football fan, I'm sorry to disappoint—when I bring up the Big Ten I'm not talking about Ohio State and Michigan. But whether you're religious or not, I hope you will appreciate the thoughts in the following passages.

The Scriptures speak directly about alternatives and marriage in several key passages. Let's look first at two of the Ten Commandments, which are the foundation of the moral law of the Old Testament:

1. You shall not commit adultery.
2. You shall not covet your neighbor's house; you shall not covet your neighbor's wife, or his male servant, or his female servant, or his ox, or his donkey, or anything that is your neighbor's [Exodus 20:14–17 ESV].

These two commandments address the sanctity of marriage—its set-apartness, if you will. The first forbids adultery—sexual faithfulness is an essential ingredient, perhaps *the* essential ingredient, in marital commitment. Sexual fidelity is something that people from all backgrounds expect in marriage.[6] Thinking seriously about another person is a warning sign of sexual infidelity.

The second commandment also speaks to how we should handle attractive alternatives. It tells us not to covet anything of our neighbor's, including his wife (or her husband).

An important passage from the Book of Malachi in the Old Testament says this: "Did he not make them one, with a portion of the Spirit in their union? And what was the one God seeking? Godly offspring. So guard yourselves in your spirit, and let none of you be faithless to the wife of your youth" (Malachi 2:15 ESV).

Even theologians with similar faiths disagree about exactly when divorce is permissible, but it's clear that divorce was not part of the original vision of what marriage could be. Of course, it's not part of people's vision for their own marriage on the day they marry. However, many divorces begin when one or both partners think the grass may be greener.

Reflect a bit more on the passage from Malachi. It says to "guard yourself in your spirit," making a profound connection between your inner life and the protection of your marriage. "Guard" in

Hebrew, *shamar,* literally means "to set a hedge of protection around something." As it relates to marriage, it means "to attend to" or "be aware" of something dangerous in order to protect your marriage.

There are many ways to guard yourself in your spirit and keep from thinking that the grass is greener on the other side of the fence. We'll explore several strategies—understanding biased perceptions, looking for weeds and noticing your own green grass, staying away from the fence, not dwelling on the greener grass, and taking care of your own lawn—to help you make the right choice.

Understanding Biased Perceptions

Let's go back now to Cindy, Martin, and Frank. Cindy had become very attracted to Frank. He offered a refuge from the pain and distance Cindy was feeling in her marriage. She became focused on what Frank did well that Martin either did not do so well or had not done recently. That's what happens when you think seriously about alternatives: you become focused on the things that the alternative appears to offer, usually failing to think clearly about the things you already have in your mate or that the alternative does not have. Hence, your perception becomes skewed.

When people marry, the person they marry has a certain number of characteristics that are on a kind of checklist we all have in our minds, whether we think about it carefully or not. Your list may be vague or specific. The items on it come from your background, your culture, and your perception of what you need. Of course, some people are only slightly aware of what they are looking for or wanting when they marry. That's why taking your time prior to marriage and carefully thinking through expectations are crucial. (Various books can help you examine your expectations before—or once you are in—marriage.[7]) But what can you do once you are married and you are attracted to someone who appears to let you check off more items on your list than your mate does?

Although you'll tend to see the items on your list that the alternative lets you check off, you will tend *not* to see the items that the person does not let you check off. Sometimes these are things that are still alive in your marriage but that you have lost track of because you haven't protected them. For example, Cindy thought that Frank was a better friend than Martin. In fact, Martin had been her best friend for years, and he remained an attentive listener. But he was not listening much to Cindy at that time. The couple had let their marriage slide, and they'd lost touch with many of the positives that had drawn them together in the first place.

This tendency to focus on what we are not getting rather than on what we have goes all the way back to Adam and Eve. With the entire wonderful garden to enjoy, Adam and Eve focused on the one thing—an attractive alternative—they could not have; they lost their perspective on all they did have. If you're also thinking that the fruit of a tree might taste great, think twice, or as many times as you need. Thinking wisely is never a waste of your time.

While Cindy was thinking that Frank might have more to offer her than Martin, the truth was that Cindy and Frank were on their best behavior with each other. They didn't have to work out budgets, discipline kids, clean up the kitchen together, or do anything hard. They could just listen and talk as friends. But it wasn't real life, and it wasn't a fair comparison. Cindy was actually more compatible with Martin, but she had lost touch with him.

You won't get far battling the temptation of alternatives if you don't recognize and accept your built-in bias. You have to push yourself to doubt your certainty that someone else could be as good or better for you. Even if you can't find anything wrong with that person, you need to recognize the importance of the promise you made before your mate, your friends, probably before your family, and, at least among those who believe, before God. The promise you made is serious stuff.

One note here before we move on: although it is often biased perception that makes an alternative seem more satisfying, it is possible to become attracted to someone who actually would be more satisfying to you than your mate. There may be something missing in your marriage that you desperately want, and although it might develop later, it also might not. It's painful to have this realization. It can also make you resentful and angry. If that's your situation, it's better to acknowledge it and grieve for the loss rather than let it erode your dedication to your mate. Otherwise, you could lose all you have built together. Dealing with this kind of grief in marriage is the focus of Chapter Nine.

Exercising Your Commitment

If you are currently attracted to someone else but you are committed to your marriage, take a hard look at how your perceptions of the other person may be biased. If the attraction is a serious threat, ask a close friend you trust to challenge you to build and maintain your commitment to your spouse.

Looking for Weeds and Noticing Your Green Grass

When you are attracted to another, you can do two things to protect yourself if you understand that your perception is biased.

First, think seriously about what's not right with the alternative. One obvious point is that you are not married to the person. Also, you, your mate, your children, and others would feel pain—and probably great loss—if you did not make the right choice.

You can also look for more specific negatives about the person. Perhaps he or she doesn't share your views on important issues, such as faith, child rearing, and lifestyle. Although your mate may not share some of your views either, it's worthwhile looking for the weeds in the other lawn—and they're there, because no one is perfect. Perhaps the other person doesn't handle money well or hasn't been responsible in his or her marriage. You don't have to demean the person, but finding the negatives will help you gain an accurate perspective and move toward appreciating what you have.

The second strategy is to think about your mate's positives and the positives in your marriage. Consider more carefully the good parts of your lawn. Very likely you and your mate have many good things together, but you may have lost track of them if your marriage has been neglected. You may want to pull out old photos and other memorabilia to help you remember what was, and likely still is, good. If you are at a low point in your marriage, be extra careful not to give in to the tendency to rewrite history and convince yourself that the positives were never there in the first place.

These two strategies amount to changing your focus from one that is unfair and biased to one that is more realistic. As Cindy began to think about her situation more clearly, she recognized that Martin did have many of the characteristics she wanted—not all, but many. But she and Martin had lost sight of much that was important. Cindy also realized they could get those things back with some work. In addition, she looked for some weeds. Frank had told her that his wife had left him because he worked so much and was never home. Well, that was what she was feeling with Martin. *Why would that be any different over time with Frank?* Cindy reasoned.

By using the two strategies, Cindy started to fight back against the thoughts about greener grass. Her dedication gave rise to her will to fight.

Staying Away from the Fence

When you are very attracted to grass that *looks* greener, you can decide to move farther away from the fence. Hanging around a fence makes it easier to see the lawn next door. Although you can't avoid being around others of the opposite sex altogether, and some of them may be attractive to you or attracted to you, you don't have to linger any longer than necessary around those you may have trouble with.

However, it may not be reasonable or possible to completely remove yourself from the presence of an attractive alternative. Take Cindy and Frank, for instance. To move completely away from Frank, Cindy would have to find another job. If her attraction to Frank was so serious that she could not resist the temptation, she would be wise to do that. On the other hand, leaving her job prematurely might leave her with a permanent image of Frank as perfect and Martin as defective. If she could resist temptation, the more powerful approach would be to work through her issues while continuing to work with Frank—finding out what's not so perfect about Frank while strengthening what she has with Martin.

If you are in a situation like Cindy's, you would be smart to get the help of a confidential friend to sort out what you are doing and why—just be sure the friend you choose is someone who roots for your marriage, or otherwise he or she will be of little help and will possibly encourage you in the wrong direction. There is plenty of room for self-deception in cases like Cindy's, so be very careful.

Let's suppose now that Cindy decides to continue working with

Frank. She still has many ways to move away from the fence without leaving the area completely. For example, she can fence off certain topics—things she will not talk about with Frank. For example, she should decide not to talk with Frank about why she is unhappy with Martin. Doing so would not only violate a boundary in her marriage but also amount to her sharing personally painful subjects with an attractive alternative, which can develop a deeper level of intimacy. She needs to resist that.

Another way to get away from the fence is to decrease the amount of time spent with the attractive alternative. Frank and Cindy have to work together a certain number of hours. They do not have to spend time together apart from work. Stopping for coffee on the way home from work, for instance, only invites trouble.

I once counseled a man who was very attracted to a woman he met at the gym. They talked as they worked out, and quite a friendship grew. But the problem for the man seemed to stem more from working out together than talking. When he thought carefully about it, he realized that although he and his wife talked quite a bit, she had never been interested in working out the way he did. It had become a source of deep resentment for him. That the other woman liked to talk was not a big deal for him. That she liked to work out with him was a really big deal.

To prevent damage to his marriage, he decided to plan his workouts so that he and the woman would not work out together. He could still say hi as he came and went, but he *planned* for them not to be together in the way that caused him the most trouble.

If your attraction to another is out in the open, you might choose to take the extra step of being overt about what you are doing. For example, Cindy could say something like this to Frank: "I know we are both dealing with some attraction here. I want to let you know that while I do find you attractive, I plan to protect my commitment to Martin. That means I have to pull back on some of the talks we've been having. I also need to pull back on some of the time we've been spending together. I enjoy it, but it's not good for my marriage. I need to keep the boundaries clearer so I can protect my marriage. I wanted to let you know so you would understand why I will be behaving differently."

If someone really pushes at your boundaries *and* you are tempted to pull the fence down, you'll have to get away from the person or risk ruining your marriage. It's your choice, and there is a right and a wrong choice.

Choosing Not to Dwell on Greener Grass

Most people feel intense desires during their life. Many of these are good and right, but many can cause you to fail in your major commitments. Although being attracted to others from time to time is likely, what is important is the extent to which you act on such attractions. Acting on them means dwelling on them, giving them a place, and letting them negatively affect your marriage.

If you have thoughts about another, you can decide not to allow them a comfortable home—you can use commitment and willpower to make the right choice. It's really up to you what happens when you deal with these dynamics. Either you will bend to your commitment or your commitment will bend to what you covet. You choose which path you take. Not challenging the what-ifs, both in your mind and in your actions, is dangerous. Guard yourself.

If you are not attracted to or thinking a lot about someone else at this time, work at keeping things that way. Watch the fences. Remain aware of how much you are thinking about others. The earlier your warning lights flash, the better.

Taking Care of Your Own Lawn

If you take really good care of the lawn where you live, the odds go down that you'll have to deal with being attracted to alternatives. That's because your marriage will stay much more rewarding, and most people are less aware of alternatives when they're happy at home. It's not enough to have a fence around your lawn that protects it from the outside. You have to work within the fence to make the lawn green and lush.

To fully protect your commitment to your marriage, you need to consistently nurture your lawn. Water it, fertilize it, rake it, trim it carefully; pull some weeds. Most lawns—though not all, I admit—respond well to tender love and care. There's often a lot of life left in even the deadest-looking lawns. But you have to bring it out. And that takes making choices and following priorities. By sanctifying time for fun, friendship, spiritual connection, physical intimacy, and all the other things that bond you and your spouse, you'll be taking care of your lawn as well as you can.

When Nancy and I bought our home, the lawn had been well cared for by the previous owner. We didn't have to exert much effort to keep it looking good. That's a lot like marriage for many of us. Early on, the lawn seems to do really well without our having to work hard on it. That's a blessing of the early stages of marriage for most people. Over the years, though, the lawn requires more effort to keep it looking the way it once did. That takes more time than it used to take. But it's time well spent.

A fulfilling marriage does not drop from heaven into your lap. It becomes fulfilling when it's tended like a beautiful garden. It won't be perfect, no matter what you do. We live in a difficult and fallen world, and we all have challenges. Because of that, the things that matter most require protection. Keeping your marriage strong and growing takes time and attention—it takes making your marriage a priority.

Some Final Thoughts on Fences and Hedges

Before we move on, I want to say a few more words on the biblical idea of setting a hedge of protection around your marriage. The nice thing about a hedge is that although it functions like a fence, it is a growing, living thing. A hedge is not a passive structure that you build and forget. You tend it. You water it. You trim it or let it grow larger in some areas for a reason. It's alive, and it can respond to the needs of the yard that it protects.

You need boundaries around your marriage that protect it and that respond to your current situation. By tending the hedge, you will be protecting your marriage and living out your dedication for the good of your marriage. That's guarding yourself in your spirit—and in your mind, body, and soul.

KEY COMMITMENT ACTIONS

- If you are currently attracted to someone other than your spouse, think of three things you can do to "stay away from the fence," and take action on them.
- Whether you are attracted to somebody else or not, discuss with your spouse several things that the two of you can do to make your marriage strong and vibrant or keep it that way. Then do them together.
- Take some time to make a list of all your mate's positive points. Then tell your mate how much you appreciate those points—and him or her. Do this often.

Now add and take your own action steps to strengthen your commitment even more:

_____

_____

_____

STEP TWO

Chapter 6

Maybe It Should Be
All About Me

When I began to study commitment in depth, I found it interesting that marriage researchers and psychologists understood the healthy dynamic of oneness in marriage in much the same way the concept is portrayed in religious teachings, especially in the Scriptures. These researchers and theorists found that commitment requires a shift from focusing on what's best for oneself to what's best for the team.[1] A strong sense of "we" is part of a growing and healthy marriage.

That's not just an interesting finding: it flies in the face of the intense emphasis on individualism that dominates our world today. Research shows that a strong marriage consists not of two separate people out for themselves but of two partners who think and act on what's best for the partnership. I call this sense of oneness *couple identity*. Its "we-ness" contrasts completely with "me-ness," or today's focus on self.

When I was in elementary school, perhaps about ten years old, I met a friend of one of my friends. A group of us went over to the boy's house to play. As I entered his garage, I noticed that each wall, left and right, was covered with a virtually identical set of gardening tools. I'm talking a lot of tools here—those people were into gardening. It struck me that each parent had a complete set of tools. It was a startling picture of separateness. It was as if each parent were saying, "Don't you touch my tools! Use your own!" I wondered then and am curious now about what that marriage was like. It could have been great. Perhaps both partners loved gardening so much that they needed all the tools. But it did make me wonder.

I'm not saying that *everything* has to be shared in a good marriage. In a strong marriage, there is some degree of separateness and a larger degree of togetherness in terms of identity and possessions. There is nothing wrong with wanting to be an individual with a clear identity. Although I don't agree with all the theories of my profession, I do agree with the commonly accepted view that many things go wrong when a person has no clearly developed sense of self.

People who have a very poorly formed sense of self are more likely to have difficulty trusting others, more likely to be insecure or arrogant, and more likely to be difficult to relate to.[2] So even as I focus on the problems of cultures that glorify self, you can be certain I'm aware that some people really do need a greater, healthier sense of self. Without it they may be hampered in their ability to learn who they can be as part of a couple. But I do not believe that this is the greatest problem for most people in marriage. If it is a problem for you, however, you will want to start dealing with it so that it does not ruin your chances at building lasting love.

Countering the Cultural Emphasis on Self

Focusing on self and not on the team is far more prevalent in some cultures than in others. In the United States, there is an extreme focus on self. From its earliest days, it has always been a nation with a strong orientation toward individualism. The Founding Fathers, who had experienced tyranny in other countries, made individual freedom a cornerstone of their new home.

But what started as respect for individual rights has steadily grown into worship of the individual. The cult of self proclaims that commitment to oneself is the highest form of commitment. In fact, if you are not committed to yourself above all else, you may be thought of as backward. These days, too many people want all the most enjoyable parts of relationships without all the hassles of commitment, dependency, and responsibility.

Intense individualism just doesn't make for a good marriage. Marriage is about commingled lives. It's about sharing and learn-ing to share more. It's about teamwork. And that sharing is benefi-cial. With greater connectedness you have someone to lift you up when you fall, to encourage you when you are low, to rejoice with you in the joys of life, and to share day-to-day experiences.

A culture that glorifies self also encourages selfishness. Focusing on "me" naturally leads to focusing on what I want, what I can get, and what you're going to give me. Although some people become mired in guilt feelings when this topic is raised—and I encourage you not to—I am convinced that it's pretty healthy to evaluate how selfish we are as we evaluate how we act in our marriage. If you think more about how you can win than about how you can give to your mate, you need to ask yourself where that attitude is coming from.

Coming Together as a Team

Randy and June started their marriage on a happy note. Both had seen a number of friends divorce young, so they had searched carefully for the right person to marry. Finding each other in their early thirties was delightful. They had both wanted to get established in their careers before they married, and they were now rising stars in their field of electrical engineering. Both were very bright and very intense about their work. Each worked a ton and probably would have made a mate miserable had they married earlier.

Randy and June are like a great many couples in our industrialized society. Although they were part of an established religion, in this case Jewish, and had grown up relatively observant in their faith, as adults they hadn't really given their faith (or God) much of a place in their lives. They were both too busy to develop a connection with a community of believers. Each was an individual and proud of it. Each was also dedicated, hardworking, and successful.

Randy and June married after dating a little more than a year. They truly did love each other, and they had a lot in common. They enjoyed discussing work and projects, and they enjoyed working out together, walking, hiking, talking, and listening to all kinds of music. And having their careers zoom along was thrilling. Life was good.

As is true for many couples in which both partners have been out on their own for years, Randy and June kept fairly separate identities after they married. Both kept their own bank accounts. They did buy a house together, however, which represented a major departure from their usual approach. Owning something together was a big step for both of them. Another big step, and a responsible decision given their priorities, was realizing that neither was interested in having children because of the time and responsibilities involved.

Neither was willing to give up what they put into their work to give children the time and attention they would need.

Five years into their marriage, two things happened that threw Randy and June for a loop. First, June's company decided to move from Denver to Houston. That sparked fireworks. Whose career was more important? Randy made it clear that leaving the firm where he was a rising star was out of the question. "I never agreed to give up my career. That's like my whole life, what I've worked for all these years!" he protested.

"But what about my career?" June demanded. "My work is just as important as yours!" She and Randy came head-to-head with a dilemma that many dual-career couples face. And neither was sure that their commitment to their marriage could compete with their commitment to their work.

Their arguments grew more frequent and more intense. June knew she had to make a decision. She was convinced that Randy was not going to move to Houston, and she felt that the future of their marriage was up to her to decide. *This is not like working through problems at work*, June noted. At work, she functioned as part of a team, which was one of the reasons why she didn't want to leave her company. The realization grew in her mind that she and Randy were not really a team. They were two individuals trying to get the most out of their lives.

Then the second thing happened. June started to feel queasy every morning. *No way*, she thought. *It can't be. We're really careful!* She went out to buy a pregnancy test kit but had to wait until the next morning to use it.

While she waited, she debated whether or not to take the test without telling Randy. She decided, *Enough of this me-versus-you business. If I'm pregnant, he's going to know about it from the start.*

When she told Randy that she planned to take the test the next morning, his initial response was not exactly gallant. He exploded and said, "That's just great. That's all we need now!" June was devastated. Randy was too, but he was unable to show it.

The next morning, the test kit worked its magic. The stick turned red, which meant pregnant. June felt blue. Randy turned green. Looking quite shaken, he said to June, "Well, there we are."

Neither of them spoke again for a very long time. Then Randy said, "What are our options?"

June's eyes filled with tears as she choked out, "What do you mean, what are *our* options? You don't mean . . . you'd do *that?*" It wasn't so much that he wanted her to have an abortion, but he desperately wanted her not to be pregnant. Life was becoming a bit too inconvenient with so many relationships and responsibilities and all this . . . this . . . *married* stuff. Although June wasn't exactly eager to have children either, neither an abortion nor adoption was a possibility in her mind. She believed that children were from God, and even though she hadn't asked for such a gift, she couldn't see how she could do anything other than move ahead.

As Randy saw June crumple on the floor in a flood of tears, he realized he had shredded her. Seeing the pain on her face, he felt ashamed that his first thoughts had been about keeping his life simple. He loved June, and moved toward her for the first time in weeks. As he hugged her, he said, "That was a stupid and selfish thing for me to say." Then he cried too, and the two sobbed and hugged on the floor for an hour.

As they sat there, Randy realized that they hadn't been this close in, well, forever. The thought startled him. He also realized that they had not faced anything tough before and that they had not had to pull together as a team.

Both June and Randy had quite an emotional day. Each went to work late, but neither got much work done. June's day was filled with anxiety about the future. *What's going to happen to me, to us, to this baby?* She felt waves of panic as she paced in her office. She also prayed. She hadn't prayed so much since the time her mother had had a cancer scare a few years before.

Randy's day was even more unpleasant. He didn't feel panic. He felt something that completely shook his sense of self. For the first time ever, he felt unsure of who he was or who he wanted to be. Everything had always been about *his* needs, *his* dreams, *his* desire to get ahead. To his credit, he did something few people ever do. He asked himself what he was living for and where he wanted to be. The possibility of an answer that wasn't framed around self-interest grew in his mind.

As many people do, even less religious people, Randy prayed, too. Somehow, thinking about God helped keep him from thinking about himself, which was especially good because he was a bit sick of what he saw when he thought about himself. He asked himself if he wanted to go through life alone—successful in his work, but alone. He decided he did not, and that meant his ideas about marriage needed to change. Randy chose to grow. Remember, commitment is always about making choices.

That evening, after dinner, he told June that he was sorry for his first response of the morning. Then, in what June thought was an amazingly humble and strong step forward, Randy said, "I've been thinking that I haven't really taken being married very seriously. So I've been looking at what that means to me, and I haven't liked what I've seen. I realize that I've wanted all the best of what we could have together without really wanting to be together. But being married is not about me or you; it needs to be about us. I don't know how to do 'us,' but I'm willing to learn."

Then Randy looked into June's eyes and said, "I don't think

we've really been married. We had a ceremony, but I don't think I have fully given myself and my future to you. I think I wanted this marriage only as long as it was good for me. I don't believe that's commitment. I want commitment. I want you to know I'll be by your side, no matter what *we* decide to do. Will you *be married with me?* I mean, you and me together."

June was shredded for the second time that day, but this time it felt much better. She felt something jump to life within her: the desire to join more deeply with Randy. After more tears and some deeply squishy hugs, the two partners started to talk a bit about *their* future. June was not sure, but she suspected that their talk that night was sprinkled with the words *we* and *our* more than they had ever been in any other discussion of their married life.

After the baby arrived, both parents were amazed at how wonderful it all was. The baby redefined for them what hard work meant, but they were doing the work together. Their change of focus from themselves to being a couple made parenting much easier and more enjoyable. It turned them into eager parents.

But what about their career dilemma? I'm not going to tell you what they did, because some of you would be upset about how it was resolved and might think I was making a broad statement about marriage. I'm going concentrate instead on the far more important point about how June and Randy turned the corner in choosing to come together as a team for the first time in their marriage.

Randy and June took what could have been the end of their marriage and turned it into the beginning of a new life together. If you did not come out of a crisis like this so well, I understand the immense pain you may be feeling. Those of us who are married face the me-versus-us dilemma almost daily, both in big and in very small decisions, and it takes fortitude to keep asking yourself, "What does this mean for *us?* How can I handle this in the best way for *us?*"

Giving to Each Other

One of the most popular and powerful writings on love is one written by the apostle Paul, recorded in the New Testament. Many religious as well as nonreligious couples have used the passage over the years on their wedding day. It speaks powerfully to the idea that love moves one to give to the other and encourages us to stay on the path of committed love.

> Love is patient and kind;
> love does not envy or boast;
> it is not arrogant or rude.
> It does not insist on its own way;
> it is not irritable or resentful;
> it does not rejoice at wrongdoing,
> but rejoices with the truth.
> Love bears all things, believes all things,
> hopes all things, endures all things.
> Love never ends.
> 1 Corinthians 13:4–8 ESV

You can be an individual, but in a strong and happy marriage you need to join your individuality with another's and give to one another, as you work together as a team.

Competition and Power

It's very difficult to become a team if you're constantly engaged in power struggles. Ponder this statement for a few minutes:

The one who is less committed has more power.

Although this idea may sound strange initially, the fact is that if one partner is less interested in being in the relationship—is less dedicated—that partner has more power because he or she cares less about what happens to or in the marriage.[3] If it's me versus you, and you are more committed to me than I am to you, then I have you over a barrel. I'm going to win.

If you walk into a dealership to look at cars and the salesperson can tell you are very interested—even committed—to leaving that day with a new car, you are dead meat. You'll pay the highest price, and the salesperson will win. Notice how good salespeople often ask, first thing, "If I can come up with a great price for you on this car today, are you really interested in making a deal?" They want to know how much leverage they have with you. If you say, either literally or in effect, "Yes, I really must have this car today. I'm totally committed to driving away today with a new car. Let's make a deal," their eyes will light up. You have less power because they know you need the car. In contrast, if you walk in and say you're merely looking and make it clear that you're not going to act rashly, you have the upper hand.

Talking about cars, let me tell you another story. In the same year that the transmission went out in our Taurus, the transmission went out in our Ford Windstar minivan—on a Sunday, right when Nancy, Kyle, Luke, and I were driving across the country. Somehow we were able to coast into the nearest Ford dealership lot, where we parked and left the car. As we left the car we noticed that there was a Toyota dealership right across the street.

Nancy had been wanting a white Toyota Sienna. Now, what do you suppose was sitting on the front lawn of the Toyota dealership? Yep, a white Sienna. OK, here's the situation. It's a Sunday. Our Windstar's transmission is ground to bits, and my wife has been wanting a white Sienna. We have two little boys, and Nancy's family is waiting for us in Canada. When we walk into the dealership, we have lots of leverage, right? Not. We were pretty much at their mercy, though I must say, the Toyota people were really good to us; they even took our Windstar, which was still under warranty, in trade on the Sienna. But we didn't have the strongest bargaining position.

The same kind of dynamic can work in marriage. For example, Carol and Bill have had a stormy marriage for twenty-four years. They argue about most major decisions because they have different approaches on issues. Their commitment has been severely tested on three occasions—and they barely survived each one.

The first crisis was about where they would live. He wanted to move across the country to take a better job, and she wanted to stay close to her family. Ultimately, she won by refusing to move with him. He was not really sure if she wouldn't go, but he decided not to test her resolve.

The second crisis was about whether they should send their kids to private or public school. Bill favored the public school, but Carol liked private, believing that it would better represent their values to their children. They went to the mat on that one too—people can become passionate when they think their children's well-being is on the line. But argue as they did, they could not resolve the issue until he threatened to leave her. She backed down. The kids went to public school.

The third crisis came in their twenty-second year of marriage when Carol's widowed mother became too frail to live on her own. She had fallen a few times while doing everyday things at home, and Carol decided that enough was enough. She convinced her mother to live with her and Bill, but it was far harder to convince Bill on the matter. Guess how she won the argument? Yep, she threatened to leave him and move in with her mother if he didn't agree to her plan.

You notice the pattern here, right? When major decisions had to be made, marital commitment became a pawn to sacrifice in order to gain the upper hand. Threatening to leave resolved each impasse, but it came with a terrible cost—the loss of the sense of commitment between two mates. Using commitment as a pawn gives one mate more power, but it undermines trust and a sense of the future, which are both crucial for a thriving marriage.

How often do you pull back on your commitment in order to gain the upper hand with your mate? Such a dynamic is the very essence of a me-versus-you, winner-loser dynamic, and it becomes stronger when you're not doing well together. It's competition in marriage at its worst. Such competition tells you that the relationship is not based on commitment.

Taking and Not Giving

It is sad when one partner is interested in oneness and the other is infected with selfishness and hyperindividualism. Peter and Mara are such a couple. They have been married for fourteen years, most of them very painful for Mara. About a year into their marriage, she realized that Peter's approach to their life together was different from her own. She felt that spouses should be equal partners, and wanted to be part of a team. He thought she should be in charge of all the household tasks while he did pretty much what he wanted to do. Occasionally he would vacuum a room or two or put the dishes in the dishwasher. But when he did even such small tasks, he was put out that he had to do them. He rarely gave her the courtesy of checking her schedule when he wanted to do something, and he'd often go over to a friend's house to play pool or watch a game at the drop of a hat. Mara found out very quickly, and very painfully, that her husband was a selfish and insensitive man.

How did she fail to see his true nature before they were married? Well, she had noticed several things that set off alarms when they were dating and engaged. But she had thought his wanting her to look after him was endearing, and she assumed that once they were married and had a home together he would become more interested in caring for it and sharing the work. It was a faulty assumption; Peter's behavior never changed.

In fact, when Mara and Peter had a baby girl, things got worse. On top of doing all the household work, Mara assumed all the responsibilities of taking care of the baby. Peter liked the idea of having a child, but he didn't spend much time with her and continued thinking only of his own needs. He also wouldn't talk with Mara when important decisions needed to be made. And sexually, well, you can imagine. He wanted and expected Mara to respond to him, but he wasn't very interested in whether or not she received any pleasure.

Mara felt dead inside. She wanted a full married life; she wanted to share everything with a loving partner. Occasionally, Peter seemed like he could be that partner—he took her out for dinner or bought her a gift that showed real thoughtfulness. But the few small gestures didn't solve the enormous issues.

How would you advise Mara? Some of you might say, *Leave the bum*. Others might say, *You don't have a good enough reason for leaving, especially with a child*. Mara's is a very tough, and not uncommon, problem.

Mara is committed to staying, and because she is, she has a couple of options to consider. One possibility is for her to seek changes in herself and hope for changes to result in Peter. Often, when one partner is committed to change, it's very hard for the other not to eventually make changes as well.

Another option is for Mara to confront Peter boldly and strongly—really get in his face, so to speak. That's what Moses' wife Zipporah did when God was about to kill Moses because he had not circumcised their son (Exodus 4:24–26). Although there is no commentary in this passage, Zipporah did save her husband's life through bold action and confrontation. Let's just say she took matters into her own hands and then was pretty confrontational about it with Moses. Dedication is sometimes quiet, but sometimes it raises Cain.

If you are walking your path without your partner's help, trying to figure out what best to do, you'll want to get support from friends and family. Go slowly and think things through carefully before you make your choice. You might also seek guidance from a counselor or leader in your faith who both respects marriage and can understand the pain of a difficult situation.

Keeping Score

Once partners start seriously scorekeeping, they are in real trouble. The problem with scorekeeping is that it is fundamentally biased in favor of the scorekeeper, which from your perspective is you. If you do a lot of scorekeeping, you are sure to score many more points than your mate.

There are many reasons for this; I'll note two. First, you see everything you do for the marriage and only a fraction of what your mate does, because you're with yourself but not your mate all the time. Second, you give yourself the benefit of the doubt while hardly ever giving the same courtesy to your mate. When things are going downhill, you may attribute the good things your mate does to chance and the bad things to character. For example, if your husband forgets to buy the ice cream you like, you might think, *He hates me; he did that on purpose just to make me mad.* Or if your wife goes out of her way to pick up a book you've been wanting at the bookstore, you might think, *OK, what's she doing now? She must want something from me.*

In books my colleagues and I have written, we call these types of thoughts negative interpretations, and warn couples that they are powerful destroyers of goodwill in marriage.[4] The bottom line is that negative interpretations make it likely that you will score little in favor of your mate once you start seriously keeping a tally. Your mate can't possibly win, and your marriage will inevitably lose.

Jake and Mindy were really into scorekeeping and making negative interpretations. Although they had been very much in love when they married, their not working as a team and letting their commitment erode had led them both to contemplate divorce. They were very unhappy, and, like most people without a strong sense of the future, they became focused on the here and now. Each tallied up what the other was doing—or not doing—for him or her.

Mindy resented how little Jake listened to her. She would come home from work and tell him about her day, and then hours later he would casually ask her about something she'd already told him about in depth. Sometimes, after they'd make a decision on something important, he would take action on the matter completely differently, following his own views instead of what they had decided together. When she demanded an explanation, he would say that he hadn't thought it would matter or, worse, that he couldn't remember what she had said. Mindy felt ignored and disrespected, and she kept a running tally of all the ways Jake let her down.

For his part, Jake thought Mindy wasn't the woman he had married. When they discussed things, she seemed aggressive and loud. It felt like she was always trying to get her way or get back at him for something, but he couldn't figure out what. He thought he always acted reasonably and nicely, and he got more and more annoyed at the way Mindy talked to him. He was very aware of every time she raised her voice or turned a discussion into an argument.

Jake and Mindy kept a close watch on how the other was "performing." Because of their biased perceptions, neither scored many points on the other's scorecard. The reality was that each was making an effort to do the things that needed to be done, but their perceptions were so biased that they continually interpreted each other's actions negatively.

As you can imagine, biased perceptions and negative interpretations put tremendous pressure on a marriage. No one fares well when these two patterns are seriously entrenched. Anger, resentment, and bitterness flow and are almost bound to increase. And when the present is unpleasant for people who see no future together, they will think a lot about divorce.

Exercising Your Commitment

Do you or your spouse engage in scorekeeping? You may not think you do, but set aside some time to talk about the issue together. Ask your partner if recent comments from you made him or her feel that you're keeping a tally of seeming faults. Discuss any issues your partner brings up, then share any times that you felt your partner was tallying up seeming missteps on your part. Ask your partner to agree that you'll both work at talking about problems rather than holding grudges or keeping score of faults. In a week, meet again and see if you both feel that the level of scorekeeping has lessened. Keep working until you both feel heard and understood.

Sacrificing

Have you ever given so much that it hurt? Have you ever put aside your self-interest for the good of another? If you are a parent, I'll bet you've done so many times for your children. But how about for your spouse? Is sacrifice relevant in marriage? I think so, but it has become more difficult to talk positively about sacrifice in our society.

Sacrifice usually involves giving up something of value—though of course not your life—to or for another. That could be your time, your pride, your money, or just about anything else you value. Sacrifice is a crucial component of commitment in a strong and healthy marriage—as long as it's properly understood.

In a healthy marriage, each partner will at times give up something more personally desirable for the good of the team. Healthy sacrifice in marriage flows most readily from a clear sense of oneness. In that context, sacrifice may be less obviously seen as sacrifice when everything is going well. Giving to your mate may not feel like giving anything up if the two of you have joined your desires and your vision for life.

Whether you are a husband or a wife, I encourage you to take the time to note what your mate does to benefit both of you, and to express your appreciation. You may be inclined to think your mate does not do much, and you could be right. But before you reach that conclusion, take a hard look at what your mate does that you may have begun to take for granted. If you're keeping score or your perceptions are biased, you are probably missing some things your mate is doing. It's especially easy to miss the small things that actually matter a great deal—making a meal, cleaning up the bathroom, fixing something broken around the house, changing one's schedule to take a child to the doctor, listening to the other's feelings about something worrisome at work, regularly praying for the other, and on and on. These things may not be a big show, but they show a big commitment.

A number of studies have been done that point out the benefits of sacrificial attitudes and actions in marriage. In my own research on commitment, I have asked people if they get pleasure out of giving to their mates. Here are some sample statements to which I ask them to respond:

> I get satisfaction out of doing things for my partner, even if it means I miss out on something I want for myself.
> It can be personally fulfilling to give up something for my partner.

My research indicates that people who are the most comfortable with the notion of sacrificing, who are most likely to say yes to these kinds of questions, tend to be the happiest, the most dedicated, and the most self-disclosing in their marriages.[5] Other researchers report much the same findings. Researchers Paul Van Lange, Caryl Rusbult, Stephen Drigotas, and their colleagues found that people who were more committed (in the manner I term *dedicated*) reported that they would give up activities that were very important to themselves individually for the sake of their relationships.[6] The researchers also found that people who were most inclined to sacrifice were the happiest in their relationships and the most likely to continue in them.

Researcher Sarah Whitton, along with me and Howard Markman, has examined the degree to which people tend to feel personal loss when making day-to-day sacrifices for their mates—for example, when performing a household task neither partner wants to do, changing their schedule to make life more convenient for their mate, changing plans for an evening or weekend because of something important to the partner, or changing a personal habit because of the partner's preference.[7] Our theory was simple: people should be most comfortable sacrificing for their partner when they have a strong commitment to the future and a solid sense of "us." What we found is that this theory works powerfully for men but only weakly for women.

What I think our finding means is that women generally sacrifice for men regardless of their certainty of their future together. Men, on the other hand, do not seem nearly as likely to sacrifice, free of resentment, unless they have committed to a future with the woman. If the finding holds up in other studies over time, it will have profound implications for our culture. As marriage deteriorates as an institution, women will receive less and less in their relationships with men because men will give their best to a woman only when they are committed to a future with her.

Giving to an Abusive Spouse

Before we go on, I want to clarify one point. I'm not suggesting that people should sacrifice their lives or put their lives in danger by remaining with someone who is a batterer. I suspect that many women stay in dangerous situations out of fear of being hunted down after they leave. However, some women remain out of commitment, either dedicated or constrained, pure and simple.

If you are religiously conservative, you may be particularly prone to staying in a dangerous marriage for the sake of commitment. (I will also point out here that, contrary to stereotype, religious couples are less likely, not more, to have problems with physical aggression.[8]) But if you are a person of faith, you might reflect on this further. I don't think anyone is called by God to remain in a physically dangerous situation for the sake of commitment or sacrifice. Furthermore, many passages in the Scriptures speak directly to the wisdom of pulling away and confronting outrageous and unacceptable behavior (for example, Matthew 18:15–17; 1 Corinthians 5). I realize that there are debates about the theology of divorce and remarriage in different situations, but no one argues that people should jeopardize their lives by remaining in a dangerous situation.

Some Final Thoughts on Giving

I am a fan of Fyodor Dostoevsky. He put these marvelous words about love and commitment and giving into the mouth of Fr. Zosima in *The Brothers Karamazov:*

> Love in action is a harsh and dreadful thing compared with love in dreams. Love in dreams is greedy for immediate action, rapidly performed and in the sight of all. Men will even give their lives if only the ordeal does not last long but is soon over, with

all looking on and applauding as though on stage. But active
love is labour and fortitude, and for some people too, perhaps,
a complete science.[9]

I don't know about love being a complete science, but I do know
that committed love often calls us to give in small ways that, in reality, are huge. The messages that swirl around in our culture don't
often reinforce making the right choices. To give up some great
personal desire or glory in order to show true, dedicated love to
your spouse is a type of sacrifice that just doesn't come up very often.
The committed life is more often about making the right choices
in the small things over time. Don't give in to believing that it's all
about you. Love does not insist on its own way. You can show this
clearly to your mate by how you handle the small opportunities that
come up each day.

KEY COMMITMENT ACTIONS

- Think about whether your sense of individualism seems
  stronger than your sense of being part of a team. If it does,
  think of three things you can do with your mate that will
  increase your feeling of being a team. Then do those things
  together.
- Think of ways you pull back on your commitment to get
  the upper hand with your mate. Resolve to eliminate any
  unhealthy competitiveness and to treat your mate fairly
  and extend your support.
- Ask your mate to tell you a specific way in which you can
  give to him or her, then do it as soon as possible. Then
  tell your mate a way that he or she can give to you. Keep
  building on the sense of sacrifice and commitment.

Now add and take your own action steps to strengthen your commitment even more:

_____

_____

_____

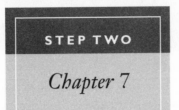

Chapter 7

Myths About Children and Divorce, Soul Mates, and Living Together Before Marriage

This chapter is divided into three parts, all of which relate to myths about family and cohabitation dynamics. We will look at divorce and its effects on children, the problems of some beliefs about soul mates, and the myth that living together before marriage increases a couple's chances of success. Why are these issues so important? Simple. If you believe things that are not really true, you may act on those beliefs in ways that harm yourself or loved ones. The three areas of belief I focus on here are everywhere in our culture and affect everyone. You may be affected by them if you do not actively, and wisely, battle against them. It is really your choice. I believe that if you are aware of such issues that you can make a more informed decision.

Maybe My Children Will Do Better If I Divorce

People who are in pain—each and every one of them—are able to talk themselves into believing things that aren't true. If you have children and you're feeling pain about your marriage, it may be tempting to believe things that may not be true concerning your children. This section of the chapter discusses what is true and what is not. It will be most helpful to those of you who are struggling with a distant and painful marriage and deciding whether or not you should stick with it. If you're not in that situation, you may want to skip this section, or you may want to read it in order to help a friend make a wise decision in the midst of a difficult period of life. Much is at stake.

Damaging Marriages

I know I have said this before, but as we discuss this topic it bears repeating: I do not believe that people should stay in destructive or dangerous marriages. I do believe there are marriages that are best ended because they are extremely damaging, and that there are others in which couples should separate until they can get a handle on things. This doesn't indicate waffling in my convictions about commitment in marriage, but rather that I recognize there can be valid reasons for people to make the agonizing decision to separate or divorce. Although I am personally conservative in my beliefs about marriage and divorce, I do believe that children living in homes in which they or one of their parents (more often the woman) is being subjected to physical danger and intimidation are *not* going to do better in life if their parents stick it out. They will, no doubt, do better if their parents are apart.

What Does the Research Show?

As a social scientist, I am fortunate to know other prominent social scientists who have focused a portion of their careers on understanding how children are affected by divorce. What I want to present here is an unvarnished look—I think a very balanced look—at the current evidence regarding how divorce affects children.

Psychological Research. I know many people who have divorced, and not one was happy to make that decision. For the sake of their children, people who are in great pain in their marriages don't usually want to divorce, and the choice to do so is usually made with agony. In the language of Chapter One, concern for the welfare of children is a major constraining force in keeping marriages together.

At the same time, with the rise in the divorce rate that began in the 1960s, there came a rise in the belief *If I'm not happy in my marriage, my children may do better if I divorce, because they will do better in life if I am not so unhappy.*

This belief is widespread, but is it valid? Part of it probably is valid. All other things being equal, most children would benefit from their parents' being happy in life. It's certainly true that children will fare best when living with both parents in a loving and happy home in which there is clear commitment to the marriage and the family. People argue about many things in academic circles, but no serious researcher or theorist now seems to doubt that children do best when raised by both parents in a loving home.[1] The hot debate among marriage experts focuses on whether or not children do better when they live in a divorced household or when they live with parents who have chronic, serious conflicts. The answer depends on the kind of social scientist you talk to.

On the psychological side, there are clearly documented negative effects on children, both boys and girls, who are exposed over the long term to parents who have significant levels of open conflict; this is one of the most profoundly clear, consistent set of findings in my field.[2] Because of these findings, some people suggest that some parents should divorce "for the sake of the children." Of course, one major problem for children whose parents do not get along well is that many of those parents don't suddenly start getting along well after they divorce. The children remain exposed to the open warfare between the two most important people in their world, and they often do not do much better even when their parents divorce.

That brings me to some advice for those of you who are married, have children, and have a lot of conflict in your marriage: learn to handle it better. You can do it, and many resources are available to help you.[3] Although you may have to swallow some pride and work at it, reducing your marital conflict is important for your children. Even if you cannot muster the motivation for the sake of your marriage—although it's better if you can do it for your marriage as well—do it for your kids. Couples *can* learn to manage conflicts better, and in doing so they can turn their marriages around and help their children.

If you are divorced and have children from that marriage, one of the best things you can do for your children is to make peace with your ex-spouse. If you are still battling, do your best to compromise and quit fighting. If you don't battle, you'll be doing your children an immense service. You want the best for them, and they need you to do this.

I realize, however, that you may believe you are right in a major dispute regarding your children, and you may feel compelled to fight for certain rights or arrangements. Or there might be abuse involved, and it is unwise to make peace with an abuser. But if what you and your former spouse are disagreeing about won't really greatly affect your children, it is much better to quit battling. Also, try not to delude yourself about what are and what are not important battles. The battling will definitely harm your children over time.

Ending your battles is of course most possible when both of you agree to "bury the hatchet" and perhaps even forgive one another. There are some thoughts about forgiveness in Chapter Nine that you might want to consider. It's not always possible to make peace with another, of course, but go as far as you can to end your conflict. If you cannot end it, go as far as you can together to shield your children from it. Doing so is essential.

Sociological Research. The other kind of research relevant to how marriage and divorce affect children is sociological. In that literature, compelling data show how much better children do when they live with both parents: they do better in school, are better off economically, are less likely to engage in precocious sexual activity, are less likely (especially boys) to become criminally involved, are more likely to stay physically healthy and have access to good health care, and are much more likely to retain a relationship with their father.[4]

It's also important to know that stepfamilies can be less than easy for children to negotiate. Although many families manage it very well, the evidence is pretty convincing that, on average, children often do not fare better in step- or blended families.[5] I know this is painful for some of you to read. Keep in mind that the research speaks to the broad average differences between groups of people, and your family can be the exception to the research findings. It's very much worth working to make it so.

To have a healthy and secure family, you need to work at and invest in your marriage, whether it's your first or a second marriage. And if you do well in the marriage you're in, your children are almost always going to do better in life.

It's also important to know that there are many single parents doing a terrific job—the information in this section is in no way a criticism of single parents or parents in blended families who are doing their best to raise their children well. My intent is to help you understand the fundamental ways in which marital stability (commitment) and harmony (getting along) provide the best environment in which your children can grow.

Now, about divorce. Many children of divorce, of course, do very well in life, showing few negative effects in their adult lives. It's quite clear from many studies, however, that divorce raises the risks for various negative outcomes for children by a factor of two to three. For example, the likelihood of children from intact homes having behavior problems is 10 percent, whereas it is roughly 30 percent for children from divorced homes.[6] So most children of divorce do not exhibit behavior problems, but the odds are significantly greater that they will. Divorce does not doom children, but children have a leg up in life if their parents have a reasonably healthy marriage and make it work.

Various findings also show that in addition to the increase in the likelihood of behavioral problems, divorce increases children's risk for other problems. Keep in mind, however, that these negative effects may well be related to divorce or to ongoing, nasty conflicts between parents or both. And it's important to remember that not all children will experience all or any of the potential problems listed here:[7]

- Greater risk for mental health problems.
- Greater risk of divorce as an adult: when one marital partner is a child of divorce, the odds of divorce for his or her marriage double. When both partners are children of divorced parents, their odds of divorce are nearly triple that of other couples.
- Greater difficulty in maintaining a good relationship with the father: 70 percent of children of divorced parents report

having a poor relationship with their father, whereas only 30 percent of those from intact homes report the same.

- Greater difficulty believing that their own marriage will last, no matter how much they want it to—this can become a self-fulfilling prophecy.
- Lower levels of educational, occupational, and financial attainment in life.
- A 2 to 2.7 times greater likelihood that they will reject their faith and religious involvement as adults compared to those whose parents did not divorce.

From what we can see here, there is no substitute for marriage when it comes to the best possible foundation for family life. Many single, divorced, and remarried adults are doing a great job raising their children, but there are many benefits from raising children within the context of a committed, and thriving, marriage.

"Good Enough" Marriages

One of my colleagues, a widely esteemed researcher at Pennsylvania State University named Paul Amato, has for years studied the long-term effects of marriage and divorce on children. Although there are several other social scientists who have done important work on this subject, including Mavis Hetherington and Judith Wallerstein,[8] I am focusing on Paul's work because of some very specific points he makes.

Paul has shown that there is such a thing as a "good enough" marriage.[9] Such a marriage is pretty good, but generally not spectacular. Good enough marriages are not passionate, not deeply fulfilling (at least much of the time), and not marriages wherein, day in and day out, the partners feel happy they found one another. In fact, in many of these marriages one or both partners often wish they had married someone else. Yet research shows that adults in these marriages as well as their children get most of the major benefits that come with family stability and support.

To Paul's way of thinking, good enough marriages usually have little overt and destructive conflict, but also little in the way of depth of connection. Their chief problem is that they are vulnerable, particularly to attractive alternatives. Good enough marriages, then, are good enough, but they are also susceptible—sort of like someone who is in basically good health but has a chronically weakened immune system. A good enough marriage that is not severely tested, such as by major health problems or by one partner's becoming attracted to a coworker, is likely to continue until one of the partners dies. All family members' lives will be the better for it—though the couple's relationship will be less rewarding than they might have hoped.

Paul has also found, from conducting a very long-term study of divorce with Alan Booth, that children of high-conflict parents tend to do better, not worse, if their parents divorce (compared to the parents staying together in chronic nastiness). In contrast, children of low-conflict marriages that end in divorce (including many good enough marriages) clearly do worse if their parents divorce. For them, the divorce usually comes out of the blue, and they are surprised, making the concept of security a mystery. When these children become adults, they tend to be commitment-phobic, bailing out of relationships at the first sign of trouble.

So, what if you are married and it's tough going? If you are in a dangerous relationship, do all that is needed to be safe. Get help and advice and support. You may need to call a domestic violence hotline. If you are in a high-conflict but nondangerous marriage, the single best thing you can do for your children is to change the pattern with your spouse by doing all you can to treat one another differently.

Exercising Your Commitment

Patterns of conflict can definitely be changed, and changing them might just save your marriage and will certainly help your children. To turn things around, get help from a counselor who knows a lot about how to help couples communicate and manage conflict more constructively. Ask a religious leader you know and respect for advice on who might effectively counsel you. The real key, though, is that you and your mate must really want to change the destructive patterns you're caught up in. Even if you are not motivated to change them right now for one another, I encourage you to do it for your children.

But what if you've been thinking about leaving your marriage for greener pastures—or pastures that appear to be greener? You may be telling yourself a lie if you're telling yourself that your children will do better if you do. To be frank, most likely your children do not care a great deal about whether you and your spouse feel passion for one another. Your children are deeply comforted by the fact, not the quality, of your marriage. Your marriage gives them a secure platform from which they can operate in the world.

I know it can be hard to hang in there when you are less than happy in your marriage. I know that for some, even huge amounts of investing are not always rewarded in their marriage. However, most positive efforts in marriage eventually do result in good things coming back to you, but not always.

If you are not so happy with your marriage, I'd like to leave you here with a bit of encouragement. (There's a good bit of advice in Chapter Eleven as well.) As part of my work with the Oklahoma Marriage Initiative, a team of national scholars devised a survey that asked twenty-three hundred adults in Oklahoma about their beliefs and experiences in marriage.[10] One set of questions asked if participants ever thought that their marriage was in such trouble that they seriously thought or talked about divorcing; 34 percent said yes. Of those people, 92 percent said that they were glad they were still together.

Think about that for a moment. We live in a culture that implies that once your marriage is down, it's out and will never be satisfying again. Yet among people who had been at a very low spot, 92 percent were glad they had stuck it out. Of course, that does not mean there are not many others who left and are glad they left. But the odds are not great that a person who divorces is going to end up happier, at least for years to come.[11]

If you choose to stick, there is hope that your marriage will get better. But for that to happen you will likely have to do some things differently—including understanding the value of marriage to your children.

Maybe I Need to Find My Soul Mate

The soul mate belief is one that affects those who are married, those who are engaged to be married, and those looking for a mate. It is an ancient idea that appeals to many. To be clear with you, I find the idea as attractive as the next person as far as what it suggests about the deepest desires of the heart—to be naked and unashamed. But is it wise to expect a soul mate? Let's take a look.

In 2001, the National Marriage Project at Rutgers University, headed by social historian Barbara Dafoe Whitehead and sociologist David Popenoe, commissioned a national survey of 1,003 people ages twenty to twenty-nine years old, 61 percent of whom had never married. In their survey, Popenoe and Whitehead asked these young adults all sorts of questions about their views on marriage and divorce. What they found will likely not surprise you, but the implications of their findings (available online at http://marriage.rutgers.edu/publicat.htm) are momentous for marriage:

- An overwhelming majority (94 percent) of never-married singles agree that "When you marry you want your spouse to be your soul mate, first and foremost."
- Less than half (42 percent) of single young adults believe that it is important to find a spouse who shares your religion. (I include this second finding simply to show that most people's desire for a soul mate has little to do with a desire to have someone share their core beliefs and spiritual practices.)

So, what is a soul mate, and why do people assume that this is the greatest thing to be desired and achieved in marriage?

Great Expectation or Dangerous Idea?
When I searched the Internet for a definition of *soul mate*, I found very few clear definitions yet plenty of writings describing what people are thinking about when they use the term. The following are some of the sentiments that I found in my search.

- A soul mate completes you.
- A soul mate accepts you no matter what.
- A soul mate has the unique capacity to love you more fully than anyone else on the planet.
- Richard Bach, who wrote *Jonathan Livingston Seagull,* suggests in part that "A soul mate is someone who has the locks to fit our keys, and the keys to fit our locks." He

further writes, "Our soul mate is someone who shares our deepest longings, our sense of direction."[12]

- A soul mate is someone for whom you would not have to make major compromises.
- A soul mate is someone with whom you have a deep connection that is not based on mere infatuation.
- A soul mate is your greatest friend.
- You *might* not spend the rest of your life with a soul mate.
- You may, in fact, have several soul mates. There is not just one.
- Soul mates have two minds, hearts, and souls that operate as one.
- A soul mate is someone you quickly know is *the* one.

As you can see, some people have soul mate concepts that are close to what just about anyone would say is a truly great marriage. Others describe (and probably seek) a level of sublime connection and completion that seems virtually impossible to achieve. Further, there is disagreement among writers: some say that there is not just one perfect soul mate for you, whereas others clearly imply that there is—one perfect person who is all-important for you to find.

One thing is clear. It is very reasonable to search for a mate who will join you in a healthy and happy marriage that will embody and portray lasting love—someone who will touch your soul. It is very reasonable to want a mate to be your best friend, your confidant, and someone who shares a deep and meaningful vision with you of your future together. I think it is not unreasonable to want and expect those things.

But not all soul mate beliefs are created equal. Some of these beliefs are so unrealistic that they put even very good marriages at risk.

Jack is such a person. He is a twenty-seven-year-old college graduate doing well in his career. Like a growing number of young people, Jack believes that you need to be financially secure and established in your career before you marry, but because he's getting to that point he has started to think about settling down.

Jack has issues, though. His parents divorced when he was seven. Both remarried unhappily, his mother once and his father twice. So he's never seen "happily ever after" in any of the marriages that have been closest to him. Yet, like most other people, he has the deep desire for the full promise of a great marriage. However, because of what he's observed up-close and personal, Jack fears that any marriage he enters into will fall far short of the promise. Sadly, his fear has a pretty serious statistical basis in reality.

But in addition to that fear, Jack has something else. Because he's a product of the current culture, he has the desire to find his soul mate if he's ever going to marry. In fact, his insecurities about marriage may have pushed him toward a desire for the fullest expression of what I call soul-mate-ism. (See the next paragraph for my definition.) Jack initially didn't believe in the whole soul mate thing, but he has grown to believe it, or rather, the belief has grown on him. The idea is comforting because he wants the most loving and secure relationship possible—something everyone wants—and he feels that he needs the perfect soul mate in order to have that happen.

So what do I mean by soul-mate-ism? Here's my definition: *Soul-mate-ism:* The belief that you will find in a mate the one unique person on the planet who understands your deepest desires and fears, accepts all of who you are unconditionally, and becomes joined to you, making one complete whole in mind, body, and soul. The power of this type of relationship is so great that you will know fully and rapidly when you find "the one." Further, if you have not married "the one," you should move on.

Soul-mate-ism is the term I use for the really dangerous form of soul mate ideology. Here's what I think is the danger.

Everyone needs to feel, and be, emotionally safe in marriage— safe in the way you relate to your mate now and safe in the sense that you can count on a future together. The danger lies in expecting an unrealistic level of sublime and safe connection. For example, in order to alleviate his insecurities about attachment, Jack needs a level of acceptance that is not possible. He needs to be fully loved, without threat of disapproval.[13]

Worse, he thinks there is only one right person who can fulfill his idea of love. That's a bit scary—such a belief implies that you had better find just the right one. I actually found a soul mate calculator on the Web that uses population statistics to tell you how many people you'd have to search among to find your soul mate— which means you could make many more mistakes than correct choices, especially if you believe there is only one right choice. What would happen if you made the wrong choice?

Pat Love, the author of *The Truth About Love*, has written a great deal about how powerfully hormones affect our thinking and feelings when we fall in love.[14] She says that our minds are taken over by the hormonal changes that occur in the early stages of new love. That's something very important to remember when you are trying to make a major decision in a wise way. So let's see what happens when someone like Jack, who's acting on soul-mate-ism, falls in love.

One fine January, Jack attended a Super Bowl party put on by his longtime friend Fred. At the party, Jack met Sandy, and the attraction was immediate. Within two days, Jack was convinced that Sandy was the one—his adherence to soul-mate-ism made him think he'd know right away. There were warning signs he should have noticed, but his strong attraction kept him from paying any serious attention to them. He thought it felt right. (Just for your information, I have nothing at all against falling in love and having it feel right.) Sandy thought so too.

Jack and Sandy are very typical. They are young and in love, and they believe what most of the people around them believe, including the idea that finding someone who shares your faith is less central than finding "the one," whether or not that person shares your faith or your worldview. The irony of most people's notion of a soul mate is that the person doesn't have to share his or her partner's most core philosophical and religious beliefs. So even though not sharing core beliefs should be a substantial warning sign of possible problems to come, it is deemed much less important than feeling you have found your soul mate. Compatible views on money management and child rearing are also very important, but may be given short shrift if you focus only on being soul mates.

Do not misunderstand me. Many partners with different faith backgrounds have developed outstandingly good marriages by any secular definition. But having different faiths is a risk, and for many couples the difference deprives them of one of the more powerful ways to meet deep in the soul.

In the area of faith, Jack's family background was Presbyterian and Sandy's was Baptist. As they spent time together and fell in love, that difference did not signify much to them because neither practiced their faith actively. They just thought about their faith in each other. And within two months they were seeing each other constantly. A few months after that, they decided to marry, and they did, with friends and family looking on.

Jack and Sandy did pretty well together for several years. In fact, they remained close and positive in their sense of a future together. Then they had a child, a girl they named Millie, after Sandy's mother. Although Millie brought them great joy and fulfillment, she also brought challenges, as children do in all marriages. Neither Sandy nor Jack had anticipated how their difference in faith would lead to so many conflicts over Millie, including how to baptize her.

But conflicts over Millie were just the beginning. Jack and Sandy also began to have conflicts about work and careers. Sandy became far more conflicted over her career once Millie arrived. She wanted to keep progressing, but she also wanted to be home taking care of Millie. It became harder and harder for Sandy to leave Millie at day care each morning. And it wasn't much better on the days when Jack was the one to drop Millie off.

Sandy began to wonder out loud about staying home and being a full-time mom until Millie was in first grade. Previously, she had not thought she would ever desire that. Yet Sandy's mother and grandmother had stayed at home to raise their children, at least in the early years. Now, though it surprised her, she thought she wanted to do that too.

Jack, however, was completely closed to that path. In fact, he felt somewhat betrayed that Sandy was even considering it because he had been sure she was as committed as he had always been to building wealth—financial security was an important component of his need to feel secure in life overall.

So a few years into their marriage, Jack and Sandy found themselves at a crossroads that is not uncommon. Nor is it particularly dangerous or threatening to a marriage. Rather, it's one of those times when married couples have to confront important choices about what they want, where they want to head, and the wisest path for them to walk on. But what made the period dangerous for Jack and Sandy was their soul-mate-ism, Jack's in particular. If Jack could feel unsafe and fear rejection or criticism in his relationship with Sandy, on any substantial level, then maybe she really was not his true soul mate. *Maybe I chose the wrong person*, he started to think.

Commitment: The Antidote to the Dangers of Soul-Mate-Ism

Soul-mate-ism conveys an expectation of heavenly connection that makes earthbound relationships more difficult. As with any other unrealistic expectation, it can make you more disappointed than is warranted by the normal ups and downs of married life. It's not that I don't believe that we should desire and seek the deepest and most meaningful connections in our marriages. And being *naked and unashamed*, as we discussed earlier in this book, reflects our desires to reach a profound level of connection in marriage. That human beings want that level of connection is the main reason I have faith that marriage will not disappear as an institution. It is the place where people are most likely to experience the level of security and safety that will satisfy the longings of their hearts.

However, there is a difference between the deepest desires of the heart, in the pristine state of the Garden of Eden, and what is realistic to expect to receive and give when married to another imperfect human being. The desire for perfection is within you and can motivate you to do greater things in your marriage, but the reality cannot come up to the level of the expectation you may have if you suffer from soul-mate-ism. So I encourage you to think well about what you expect so that you will not be unhappy with your marriage because of impossible expectations about being perfectly loved by another.

The desire we all have to be fully and deeply accepted and connected—implied in the words *naked and unashamed*—can be fulfilled in the context of full commitment. It is deep commitment between two partners for life in marriage that makes it possible to have a profound connection.

For Those Who Are Searching for Their Soul Mate

Most of what I have written in this section is for those of you who are not married but who are seeking a mate or think you have found the right one. If you are married to someone but searching or longing for the soul mate you believe you did not marry, my core advice is in much of the rest of the book; Chapter Eleven may be particularly helpful. Go very slowly. You can lose a great deal very rapidly when you are unhappy and act rashly. I do wish you all the wisdom in the world in handling the pain of your current situation.

But for those of you who are looking to marry, I think that there is an aspect of the belief in soul mates that can be especially beneficial: having a soul mate supports the notion of searching for a soul mate.

For decades, researchers have said that an adequate search is an important part of creating a good marriage. The notion is that people are most likely to do well in marriage if they have searched enough to make a good choice. The implication—and various findings support this—is that you can marry someone before you've looked hard at all the choices, and that choosing without looking hard enough means you can miss the best match.

This may be why some online matching services embrace the soul mate idea so strongly. First, it speaks to what people want. Second, it supports the idea that a matching service might be a good option to pursue. Not to name names, but I think that ad campaigns that strengthen soul mate ideology in our culture are generally not a good thing. Yet I have come to believe that matching services can be very effective for some people for one simple reason: the good ones allow you to sort among choices according to the values, beliefs, and interests you say are most important to you in a mate *before* you actually meet potential mates and perhaps fall in love—before all those hormones Pat Love writes about get in the way. Once that happens, your thinking may not be so clear, and your hormones may convince you that a person is your soul mate when the two of you are actually not very compatible.

Although I believe that what you do after you marry is the most crucial factor in being successful in life, I and other marriage researchers also believe that making a wise, careful, unrushed choice up front is the very best way to begin a life with another. At the end of this chapter, after the next section, I present some basic guidelines for those of you who are looking for a mate and contemplating marriage. I also talk about some related themes in the following section on living together before marriage.

Maybe We Should Live Together First

In recent years, I've been involved in research on living together prior to marriage. In fact, one of the things my team and I have been doing is working to understand the findings in this area through a strong perspective of commitment.

One of my most important colleagues is Galena Kline. She's a brilliant researcher who is particularly interested in cohabitation dynamics. So I am going to do something different with this topic. I've asked Galena to write this section, for a number of reasons.

First of all, she's a lot younger than I am. In addition, she is quite liberal minded where I am conservative and religious. Why does this matter? Because I think it's likely that those of you who will be most interested in this section will be younger and maybe more liberal than I am, contemplating the pros and cons of living together prior to marriage. So you should hear what the research says from someone who is more like you.

However, I am going to add some thoughts of my own to Galena's summary; you'll see my commentary inserted in brackets.

In that way you'll hear what she's saying and also what I'm saying. You'll get a very complete perspective, no matter what your personal beliefs. Then you can decide what all the information means to your life.

❧

Galena Kline's Summary

In the last fifty years, more and more people have started living together outside of commitment to marriage. In fact, 60 percent or more of couples now live together before they get married, and many others live together instead of getting married. The rates of living together are even higher for remarriages. Many believe that living together is a good way to "test" the relationship or give it a trial run. Perhaps because they are either wary of commitment or have particular reasons to be concerned about their relationships, many think they will learn things about their relationship that will help them decide whether to commit to marriage with a particular partner.

The majority of young adults do believe that living together helps people make decisions about marriage as well as provides a way for couples to work through issues before making a lifelong commitment. In fact, over half of younger people believe that living together prior to marriage will lower their odds of marital problems and divorce.[15] Research, however, suggests something quite different.

? Did You Know . . .

- People who lived together before marriage have a higher rate of divorce than those who did not live together.
- People who lived together before marriage report that it is

more likely they will divorce than people who did not live together.

- People who lived together before marriage have more negative communication in their marriages than those who did not live together.
- People who lived together before marriage have lower levels of marital satisfaction than those who did not live together.
- Infidelity during marriage is more common among people who lived together prior to marriage than those who did not.
- Physical aggression is more common among married individuals who lived together before marriage than those who did not.

There are always exceptions to any research findings, but there are many studies documenting these important differences.[16] Researchers disagree only on what these findings mean, not on the fact that the findings show up in study after study.

Is It All About Commitment? In a recent study conducted by my research group, we found that it mattered a great deal whether couples had clear plans to marry before starting to live together.[17] As part of the study, we examined the relationships of 136 couples, asking both partners to complete questionnaires and videotaping the couples discussing a problem. We also looked at their relationships just before marriage and soon after. We split them into three groups: those who lived together before getting engaged, those who lived together after engagement but before marriage, and those who didn't live together until they got married.

Here's what we found: couples who lived together prior to being engaged were most likely to experience difficulties in their relationships both before marriage and about a year into marriage. They had lower satisfaction, poorer communication, more conflict, higher rates of physical violence, and less confidence in their relationships than people who waited until after they were engaged or married to move in together.

Although we will need to conduct more research with other samples before we can say that what we found with this sample is definitively the case, the finding was very strong, suggesting that if a couple is clear about marriage before moving in together, their chances for marital success may be equal to people who wait until marriage to live together. At the very least, people who are engaged when they move in together do not seem to be as greatly at risk as those who move in together without clear intentions to marry.

[Scott: In a much larger sample, some differences between those who were engaged at the time they moved in together and those who waited until marriage might be statistically significant, with those who wait until marriage probably doing best of all groups. But as Galena states, neither of those groups of couples had anything like the risks of the couples who moved in together prior to deciding they wanted to marry.]

Another key finding from work done by Scott and his colleagues relates to interpersonal commitment, or what he has been calling dedication throughout this book. A study conducted with a national random sample found that those who had lived together prior to marriage were less interpersonally committed later on in their marriages than people who hadn't lived together before marriage.[18]

But here's an important point: this finding was true only for men. Men were less dedicated in their marriages if they had lived with their partners before marriage. This finding was recently confirmed in another large survey as well.[19]

[Scott: Commitment levels, especially related to my definition of dedication, have only recently been measured in studies on living together prior to marriage, but all the assessments we know of have come out this way. However, all research findings are based on averages in large groups, and it's important to realize that there are always many exceptions to the strongest research findings. So not all marriages in which the couple lived together prior to marriage have less dedicated males, only some. But the overall pattern runs clearly in this direction.

We also have found that the males who are least likely to live with their wives prior to marriage are more religious. In contrast, how religious the females are seems not to matter at all, at least in my study that Galena refers to. However, for males, religious differences do not explain the differences in levels of dedication. In other words, both differences hold up in analyses.]

What does this mean? It means that men might be less willing to work at marriage if they've lived with a spouse before getting married.

Why Does Living Together First Often Result in Negative Outcomes? There are several theories about why living together is associated with more negative outcomes for couples. Here I'll cover a handful that I think are most important.

First, some people believe there is something important about the experience of cohabitation that relates to a higher risk of divorce (the *experience theory*). What might that "something" be? Well, some have found that people's attitudes about marriage and childbearing change—become more negative—after living together.[20] So it could be that living together makes people less interested in marriage and less interested in having children. Others have speculated, however, that when people live together they develop a mind-set in which they think, "Well, if this doesn't work, I can easily get out." The problem is that this mind-set might not change when the couple gets married, making it easier for them to divorce.

Other experts believe that it's not actually the experience of living together that relates to poorer outcomes over time, but rather that people who live together before marriage already have characteristics that put them at risk for divorce and unsatisfying marriages (the *selectivity theory*). A host of research indicates that there are important differences between the backgrounds of people who live together before marriage and the backgrounds of those who don't. For example, those who live together before marriage are, on average, less religious, less educated, less well off economically, less traditional in their values about marriage and children, and more likely to be from divorced families, and they tend to have a larger difference between their ages than couples who wait until marriage.[21] According to this theory, then, living together does not itself make marriage riskier for couples; the couples are already at higher risk.

Because of these findings, some have tested to see whether differences in backgrounds can account for the finding that living together before marriage is associated with higher risk for divorce. In the two studies conducted by our research group, as well as in studies done by others,[22] statistically controlling for these differences did not change the results. So there has to be something more.

Scott, our colleague Howard Markman, and I have done a lot of thinking about this. None of us thinks that either the experience theory or the selectivity theory captures everything about living together. Some of their points are likely to be true, but we think that commitment must also be considered, as well as individuals' initial reasons for cohabitation—two things that other theories don't take into account and that have actually received very little attention from researchers so far.

[Scott: Galena's particular research interest is examining, in detail, the who and why of living together (or not) prior to marriage. What are people thinking when they decide to live together? How many people make the decision because it merely seems convenient? How many make it because they are afraid of losing the person they are with? How many sense problems in their relationship and want to test it by living together? Understanding these factors will advance the field a great deal.]

Our main theory, which we call the *inertia theory*, is simple. It suggests that external pressure to remain together starts to build when a couple moves in together. You move in together, buy a place, get a dog, spend less time with friends and more time alone together, and maybe declare the other as your beneficiary for financial matters—and these things make it more likely that you will stay together. In other words, there is an increasing weight of forces that favor your staying together when you live together. In the words of Scott's commitment theory, living together increases constraints, making it harder to leave a relationship.

Something that too few people recognize is that it's hard to end a relationship with someone when you share things like a home, possessions, and friends. We chose *inertia* to describe our theory because it implies that partners who are living together may stay in their relationship, on a path toward marriage, unless a major force derails them.

[Scott: We first speculated about the inertia concept after finding that husbands in marriages in which the couple lived together beforehand tended to be, on average, less dedicated to their wives than husbands who had not lived with their wives prior to marriage.[23] Since that time, we have puzzled over why men who cohabited prior to marriage would be less dedicated. Gradually, we began to suspect that it is because some men were less dedicated to their female partners all along and that many of these men would

not have married the woman they were married to if forces had not pushed them—forces that the fact of living together increases (constraints). These couples are sliding, not deciding, their way into marriage.]

Here's an example. Todd and Lorraine were in their mid-twenties when they met. They dated for a few months, and when Lorraine's lease ran out, she moved into Todd's place. *I'm spending most of my time with Todd anyway,* Lorraine thought, and she already kept many of her clothes and other things at his place.

When she moved in, she and Todd signed a new one-year lease together, and she paid for half the deposit. Then they decided to get a puppy. And when Todd's car broke down, it seemed to make sense for him and Lorraine to buy a car together. She provided the down payment and then they split the monthly payments.

All these seemingly minor steps would make it harder for Todd and Lorraine to end their relationship if either decided that that was what he or she would prefer to do. If they each kept their own place and dated exclusively and regularly, it might be painful to end the relationship but far easier than it would be once they started living together.

The key here is to think about what is happening with commitment. If Lorraine and Todd already know they are dedicated to each other and to marriage in the future, especially if they are engaged, then the pressures to stay together that come with living together will not really affect their path. Those pressures won't be the reason they end up marrying. Living together may increase some of their other risks, such as by eroding their belief that marriage illustrates the highest form of commitment, and that's not good. But living together would not make it more likely than it already was that they would marry.

But let's change the scenario a little. Suppose Todd and Lorraine are very emotionally attached but not at all clear about their future.

In fact, suppose that although they are attracted and interested, they each have some concerns about their relationship (say, they argue a lot, and sometimes these fights nearly get physical) or about one another (perhaps Todd drinks a little too much or Lorraine has serious problems holding onto a job). Now it's a very different story. Sure, they are living together because they want to spend more time together, but it's also because they want to test the relationship.

[Scott: The inertia theory suggests that couples who are at the greatest risk are those who are in love but aren't sure they want a future together. People don't realize that it's much harder to break off the relationship once they move in together. Further, many couples have children (planned or not) when they live together,[24] and that makes it even more gut wrenching to contemplate ending the relationship.]

Now let's look at a couple who planned to marry before they moved in together. Brian and Bree, both in their early thirties, started talking about getting married after they'd been dating for about nine months. He romantically asked her to marry him while they were visiting the Grand Canyon, and she said yes.

When Bree's lease was up a couple of months later, they decided it made sense for them to move in together, in part to save money for their wedding and first home and in part because they wanted to spend more time together. They signed the lease together, got a cat, and bought a car.

Have they increased their risk for a poor relationship? Most likely not. This couple is on the path to marriage and, in all probability, would have gotten married whether they lived together or not. So for them living together did not increase the chances of a higher-risk relationship.

[Scott: My more conservative bent makes me have a different take on this scenario. I think it's simply safer and clearer to wait until marriage to move in together. I realize that many engaged couples cite the convenience

of living together, often just a month or two before the wedding, but research findings make a pretty good commercial for the notion that the "old-fashioned" way is wiser. Furthermore, if you are not married, it's possible to convince yourself that "this is the one" and that the person you're living with will surely eventually want to marry you. That way of thinking is very dangerous.]

Let's look at another scenario involving a couple in their mid-twenties. After Greta and Dan had been dating for a few months, Greta's lease ran out, and Dan casually asked her to move in to save money. She agreed. As is very often the case, this couple didn't talk seriously about the decision to move in together; it "just sort of happened."[25] They started living together without a clear plan to marry.

But now that they are living together, Greta isn't so sure she wants to be with Dan for the long haul. He drinks more than she does, and he likes to go out with friends and party. They argue a lot about money. Still, Greta tells herself, it's fine for now.

Nine months later, Greta is getting fed up. She has realized she wants to get married and start a family, but Dan has said he's not ready. They start arguing even more. Greta wants to break up, but decides to wait until the lease is up. She doesn't want to make life difficult for Dan, and it's going to be hard for her to afford a place on her own. But just before the lease is up, things get a little better between them and Greta unexpectedly gets pregnant. Once she is pregnant, she really wants to get married, and Dan eventually agrees.

Unlike in the previous scenario, here the risks of living together are important. That's because this couple probably would not have gotten married if they hadn't lived together. Constraints, not dedication, have propelled them forward.

[Scott: Greta and Dan are a perfect example of something I think happens far too often: people marrying because they were living together even though the man never fully committed—sliding versus deciding. I call these

"maybe I do" marriages because the couples do not express a clear "I do" on their wedding day. My advice here, to both women and men, is that if you have to drag your partner to the altar, it is probably an indication of many draggings to come. A mate who commits reluctantly is less likely to be a dedicated partner in marriage.

When you live together prior to marriage or engagement, you are giving up options before you've clearly made your choice. Life almost never turns out as well when you give up options before choosing.]

What If You Want to Test the Relationship? If you're thinking about moving in together because you want to test your relationship, you're probably better off testing it in a way that doesn't make it harder to break up. If you aren't both ready to commit to marriage, I think you should wait.

[Scott: I believe that the surest way to test the relationship and know whether your partner is committed to you for life is to see if he or she makes it all the way to the altar before you move in together. Old-fashioned, I know, but it is so very, very clear that way. As a researcher, I believe that Galena is right about risks being very much lower for those who are engaged. Keep in mind, though, that this is an idea based only on research. You need to think about the other dimension of values and beliefs, including religious beliefs. One of the most important things that nearly anyone who knows these data well now agrees on is that living together before marriage cannot be said to have the benefits that most young people in particular have been led to believe it has.

One other thing about tests. Choose low-cost tests, not high-cost tests. Living with someone, buying things, becoming pregnant, and so many of the things that come with cohabitation prior to marriage are very high-cost tests of the viability of your relationship. Chose lower-cost tests such as reading a book (like this one) together and thinking through how you each see life together. Or take a workshop together. Will your partner

go? Take on some project together (other than setting up house), like doing
something for the poor. Do things that are real tests of compatibility, not
false tests with a high risk of putting you on a path for risk in marriage.]

So if living together isn't a good way to test a relationship, how
do you test it? First, it's important to really consider why you want
to test it. Two common reasons are that you have serious concerns
about your partner or relationship or that you are generally a wary
individual but don't have specific concerns. Examples of the first
category might be that your partner's having mental health issues
that make you unsure about marriage to him or her, your partner
drinks too much, you and your partner have physical fights, you
cannot see yourself with this person for the long haul, or you fight
frequently and destructively. All these factors have to do with your
being unsure of your partner both as a person and a future mate.

People in the second category might want to test for other reasons. Maybe they grew up in a divorced home and feel they don't
understand what lifelong love looks like. Or they may have been
seriously burned in previous relationships—perhaps someone they
loved cheated on them or left them unexpectedly. These people are
less sure of themselves or of love and commitment in general, and
may be especially anxious about whether or not a partner would
really accept them and never leave.

If you fit into the first category, it's very important that you carefully assess your relationship and avoid making commitments that will
make it difficult to get out of an unhealthy relationship. For example, don't buy expensive items with someone you might want to
break up with. Have conversations about these issues with your partner and think about what you need in a mate. Ask people you trust,
such as friends and family members, what they think—they might
be seeing problems too. The same people are likely to support you
if you decide to end the relationship.

If you fit into the second category, you might need to do some work on your own to figure out where the difficulties come from and how to get past them. Think about whether your partner is consistent enough in his or her commitment to relieve some of your anxiety about the long term. If you are anxious about attachment, resist the temptation to hang onto people who may not be very good for you or to press for living together in order to feel more secure. You want to look for a mate who is exceptionally clear and consistent in his or her commitment to you, and living together prior to marriage is unlikely to give you any useful information about this. But do give your partner a chance to show commitment to you. Sometimes people get so caught up in searching for someone who will be wholly committed that they miss the simple ways their partners show they care.

If you're in either category, it's wise to take things slowly. Give yourself the opportunity to figure out just why you want to test the relationship before you commit to marriage.

Mate Selection 101

Surprisingly, marriage scholars and researchers have not devoted a great deal of attention over the past decades to good mate selection. Sociologist Norval Glenn at the University of Texas has noted that this is a serious gap in the field, and I think he is right. Simply put, we need to discover more than we know, but couples can also benefit right now from what we've learned already.[26]

I will close this chapter by presenting a very simple list based on many years of research, of counseling couples, and of reading and thinking about this issue. The more of these suggestions you are able to follow when you are searching for a mate and thinking about marriage, the better your odds will be of making a wise choice.

- Get to know the person very well before deciding to marry. One thing you can do is take the time to work together through a detailed list of core expectations to see just how compatible you are. (For guidelines on how to do this, you might check out one of the books I've coauthored.[27])
- Do not make this crucial decision in a period of emotional infatuation.
- Date the person for a long time.
- Observe how the person treats not only you but also his or her friends. Learn as much as you can about the person's priorities and values.
- Give more weight than your heart may want to how closely the person shares your most essential beliefs (including religious) and values in life.
- Wait until you are twenty-two or older to make such an important decision. What you think you are looking for can change a lot.
- Get the opinion of friends and family who are not likely to tell you only what you want to hear.
- Wait until you are married to live together. It may or may not increase your risk to do otherwise, but there is no evidence that it will increase your risk to wait.

∾

This chapter has covered a lot of ground. If any of the major myths we've discussed are affecting your life and choices now, I hope you will give a lot of thought to the ideas Galena and I have presented. I know it's not my job to tell you what to do with your life, but it is a mission of mine to help people understand how various beliefs and decisions might affect them and those they love. The best decisions come from the clearest thinking.

⚷ KEY COMMITMENT ACTIONS

- Do you suffer from soul-mate-ism? If you think you do, think carefully about that expectation, try to develop a more realistic belief about marriage, and work on bringing unrealistic expectations of your mate down to a real-life level.
- If you are living with a partner but not yet married, think of any external pressures, such as owning a pet or a home together, that might be influencing your thoughts of marriage. If you're not sure whether you're remaining in the relationship because of pressures of constraint or dedication, talk with a few close friends or relatives to hear their take on your relationship.
- How comfortable are you with your partner's commitment level? Look for, and write down, ways that he or she is showing commitment to you and your relationship. Look for small things, such as planning future things to do together, as well as more major signs of commitment. If you are unmarried but thinking about marrying someone, also make sure you consider evidence that he or she is not really committed to you.

Now add and take your own action steps to strengthen your commitment even more:

_____

_____

_____

STEP THREE

Building Your Future with the Power of Commitment

The way we conceive the future sculpts the present,
gives contour and tone to nearly every action and
thought through the day. If our sense of future is weak,
we live listlessly.

EUGENE PETERSON

Goal of Step Three: In this step, we will focus on the actions you can take to experience the full power of commitment to build and maintain the best of life together.

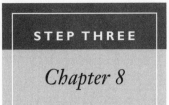

Chapter 8

Living with an Eye to the Future

It was a time of unparalleled darkness. In 1929, the Great Depression shook the lives of both the rich and the poor, and continued to do so for the decade that followed. Then things got worse. The financial uncertainty of the Depression gave way to a greater fear—the possibility of war. The whole Western world seemed to be coming unglued.

Most of the time when we think of vision, we think of something positive. But it's also possible to have a dark vision. Adolf Hitler was a man of dark vision. He rose to the height of his power with the help of the Depression. The German people had been suffering terribly. Their economy was in shambles; fathers and mothers could not work hard enough or fast enough to feed their children. The people also continued to feel the sting of defeat from World

War I. The road was paved for Hitler's vision of national glory and domination. Among other things, he convinced many Germans that their suffering was the result of a Jewish and Communist plot. He captivated the nation with his powerful vision of blinding hatred, raw power, and superiority.

Adolf Hitler had a dark heart and a dark vision, as many of his statements clearly reveal. The following are just a few examples:

> "Any alliance whose purpose is not the intention to wage war is senseless and useless."
> "Success is the sole earthly judge of right or wrong."
> "A violently active, dominating, intrepid, brutal youth—that is what I am after. . . . I will have no intellectual training. Knowledge is ruin to my young men."[1]

Imagine living through those years. Perhaps you don't have to imagine; you only have to remember. The economy of your land was in rubble. All around there was nothing but uncertainty. Within that culture of fear, Hitler and his vision arose in one of the most powerful nations on earth. From 1933 on, Hitler rebuilt Germany into a military powerhouse. Nearby nations feared his ambitions, and other countries took comfort in their distance. Within Germany, Hitler's foes were defeated easily, and he steadily gained political power.

Where would you have looked for hope? Perhaps you would have looked to the United States, but the country was isolated from the world at that time. England, led by Sir Neville Chamberlain, had an official policy of appeasement with the slogan of "Peace for our time." Although I am sure many people had the foresight to see where things were headed, one man in history spoke out—loudly. He had a different vision from Hitler's, but he, too, understood the power of a vision. He saw what was coming, and he saw what was needed. His name was Sir Winston Churchill.

Churchill argued for years that England needed to rebuild and vitalize its military, especially its navy. He could see the storm coming from Europe, and he openly criticized his nation's policy of appeasement. Churchill said of appeasement, "An appeaser is one who feeds a crocodile, hoping it will eat him last."[2] In essence, Churchill took the long view while other world leaders held on to the short-term hope of appeasement.

Germany began World War II with a tremendous advantage in both military and material might. But Churchill inspired his people. Even though the country was outgunned, he gave the British people a vision of a future of victory, freedom, and honor. His vision gave the free world something more powerful than military might. He inspired people to overcome fear and to fight and, if necessary, to die for what was right.

The contrast between Churchill's words and Hitler's is striking. Earlier in his career, Churchill stated, "Sure I am of this, that you have only to endure to conquer. You have only to persevere to save yourselves."[3] Later Churchill declared, "Let us therefore brace ourselves to our duty, and so bear ourselves that if the British Empire and its Commonwealth last for a thousand years, men will still say, 'This was their finest hour.'"[4] Churchill made the last statement in a speech to the House of Commons at the beginning of the Battle of Britain. During the following months, the people of England found within themselves the ability to fight far beyond their obvious resources.

Hitler knew the power of a vision of domination, but he vastly underestimated the power of England's vision of freedom from oppression. The people of England were inspired, both by the immensity of the task at hand and by the words of their leader. *That's what a good vision does—it inspires you to live to your fullest potential. A good vision helps you transcend what keeps you from living abundantly.* It pulls you toward the higher objectives in life.

Hitler had a vision that was dark and evil. Churchill had a vision filled with confidence, hope, resolve, and dedication. Each leader pulled his nation forward by the power of his vision. Both visions were powerful. One was right.

What does it mean to have a right, powerful vision for your marriage? That's what I hope to explain in the rest of this chapter, because having the right vision in your marriage can help you conquer the forces working against the two of you living life to the full. If you want to really live out the power of commitment, you need to nurture a vision for your life together.

What Exactly Is a Vision?

A vision is an image or ideal that guides people, often providing meaning, motivation, and inspiration for the tasks ahead. A good vision includes elements of foresight, idealism, and dedication. A vision is more than seeing a certain kind of future; it is seeing the future so clearly that you act on it.

I didn't relate the story about World War II visions because I think of marriage in terms of war. I pointed to Churchill and Hitler as examples of the power of vision. Having the right vision is an essential element in living out your commitment. Vision is necessary in a strong marriage, but the wrong kind of vision will keep you from a strong and thriving marriage. The prevalent vision of marriage today is not one that inspires many people.

Positive Vision or Cynicism?

Solomon asserted, in Proverbs 29:18, that without vision we perish. Why *perish?* Because the larger view gives meaning to the details of life that otherwise can diminish your soul. Grand visions inspire us to higher ideals and values, without which we are all vulnerable to the ravages of cynicism. Never before have a people had so much wealth and so many opportunities as we do, but do we see a land flowing with optimism and goodwill? No. The pervasive attitude says believe nothing, trust no one, and live for the moment. That's not a positive vision to inspire people. It's a selfish, cynical vision that kills the soul. With regard to marriage, this dark vision shouts out,

- Marriage does not work.
- Marriage is temporary.
- Marriage is for romantic fools who think they can make love last.
- Marriage is a trap used by men to confine women to lives of slavery.
- Marriage is a trap used by women to confine men.
- Marriage constrains your capacity to enjoy and express your sexuality.
- Marriage will keep you from realizing your full potential.
- Marriage institutionalizes men's abuse of women.
- Married people are less satisfied in life than unmarried people.

The message underlying all these statements is that commitment in marriage is unrealistic, if not completely stupid. Have you heard these messages in the news, in the movies, in popular music, from your friends?

Most people who stick with marriage experience huge benefits from it. But unless you work to the contrary, the vision you are likely to have for your marriage is the one handed to you by your culture. Is that the vision you want to guide you in your marriage?

What Is a Realistic View of Marriage?

The view that marriage is irrelevant at best and harmful at worst is common, but it's not the view that we should accept. Nor is it a view that we should ignore. The fact is, such cynicism has some validity—it reflects what all too many people have actually experienced or seen others experience. Even though the cynicism is understandable, however, marriage *does* have immense value, and it is worth the effort it requires.

Did You Know . . .

People have become cynical about marriage for a number of good reasons. Among them are the following facts, which make it that much harder to maintain a positive vision. For the good of your marriage, you need to keep an affirmative vision despite these trends.

- One out of every two young couples who marry for the first time will divorce.[5]
- Our media-driven culture rarely presents images of good marriages.
- In the United States, more children are born to young women who are unmarried than to those who are married; childbearing is becoming increasingly disconnected from marriage.[6]

- Although the number of children born out of wedlock has decreased slightly in recent years among teens, the rate over-all remains very high: about 32 percent of all births in the United States in 2000 were out of wedlock compared to only 6 percent four decades earlier.[7]
- The percentage of married people who say they are very happy has declined over the past three decades. This is proba-bly due to how unrealistic people's expectations have become for marriage, making them less satisfied than they used to be even when things are pretty good.[8]
- Most young people, especially females, have somehow been convinced that marriage has no bearing on how they will do in life, when mountains of research suggest just the opposite.[9]

Sure, there are some marriages that virtually none of us would think it wise to continue. But far more often, marriages are the very best long-term investments that people can make. Marriages can be risky for people, yet life is even riskier without marriage—riskier for individuals and for society.

If you are inclined toward the cynical vision of marriage, I want to ask you to reconsider and to think through what kind of impact this view can have on society and on your life. There is a mountain of scientific evidence showing that a committed, strong, and safe marriage is good—good for you, good for your children, and good for society.[10]

Good marriages result in better opportunities for children, better social connection among adults, family financial security, fewer risks for mental health problems, better physical health, and even more satisfying sex. Not exactly in keeping with the dominant worldview, is it? Although the overall benefits of marriage are greater for men (on average), the benefits are clearly in evidence for both men and women. Most people who stick with it experience huge benefits.

One caution before we move on. It is possible to develop views of marriage that are wildly unrealistic, almost fantasylike, and that thereby encourage greater feelings of disappointment. It is also possible to accept a lower, more cynical view of marriage, but doing so will virtually guarantee that your marriage becomes a hollow shell. Be careful. Try to achieve a *positive, full, realistic* vision of what you can develop together in your marriage.

What Are You Building?

Winston Churchill spoke on many subjects, not just war. One of the things he said was, "We shape our buildings: thereafter they shape us."[11] Building a marriage is much like building a house, and the plans you follow are shaped by the vision you have in mind. The vision you construct for your marriage will shape the life you have.

All couples have some model in mind for marriage. In fact, each individual in a marriage has a vision, but that vision may not be shared by the other person. Some couples have a shared vision that guides them wisely as they construct their relationship. Others have a vision that is more infected by the culture—a vision of foreboding and helplessness. Although it's hard for me to imagine, I suppose there are some couples who have no vision at all, not together as a couple and not as individuals. This is not to say that they don't have any expectations. We all do. But they have no view of life and marriage that's bigger than the events of the day. The ideal is to have a shared, positive vision for your future together.

Let's go back to the two couples we met in Chapter One. Take a few minutes to read again about Jeremy and Suzanne and Lisa and

> **Exercising Your Commitment**
>
> Do you have a shared vision for your marriage? Talk with your partner about things that are important to both of you that you can use as a blueprint by which to build your relationship. Talk, for example, about values, philosophies, and the level of dedication you want to see in your marriage, rather than about possessions you hope to obtain. Create a full, positive ideal for your marriage but make sure that the vision is realistic and achievable.

Steven. Jeremy and Suzanne came to their marriage with a strong, positive, and committed vision for their future. They shared this vision, and they were guided by it as they began to build their life together.

Contrast that with Lisa's vision of foreboding. She had a vision, but it was more of a nightmare than a vision to propel her forward. She wanted desperately to have hope and a positive vision, but even her mother had little hope to offer her. In a way, Lisa's vision was mixed. On the positive side, she knew what she wanted: a full, life-long commitment in marriage. But her positive vision was obscured by dark clouds that came from the failed dreams of so many couples around her—she knew more couples who had divorced than who were making it work. She wanted to believe that the higher view was possible, but she was neither sure nor easily reassured.

I think Lisa and, I hope, Steven have more going for them than those without any vision at all. The couples who concern me most aren't even thinking about having a vision or about what they are trying to build. They are plodding along with whatever model of marriage was given to them by their backgrounds and culture, and are not particularly inspired about anything beyond that. For more and more couples, the vision of being together doesn't include marriage, just living together as long as it's convenient. But the commitment level of those who live together and who have no plans for marriage are much more like that of dating couples than of married couples.[12] Cohabitation is not the same as marriage.

Lisa was troubled in a way that is good. She was struggling with the disconnect between her deeper desires for marriage and the realities of the marriages she had seen. Struggling is good because thoughtful people make considered choices. From all the work I have done in the field of marriage, I am convinced that if the average couple thought more carefully about the commitment they were making and waited six more months before they married, the number of divorces would go down substantially. Too many people don't reflect enough on what they are doing and why they are doing it.

You can be different. You probably *are* different, or you wouldn't be reading this book. Having said that, I want to encourage you to work at fully developing a positive vision for your marriage. Such a vision can hold in check the cynicism of our day. Your marriage is meaningful and is worth fighting for and working on. Developing a positive vision is a powerful way not to get stuck.

Nurturing Your Positive Vision

Mates who consistently nurture a vision for their life together are the most likely to have lifelong, happy marriages. Fran Dickson at the University of Denver has studied couples who have been married for fifty years and more.[13] In her research, she found that happier couples reported talking regularly about their future over the years. Further, those who were together and happy later in life—those who were sticking—had this sense of vision, whereas those who were together but relatively unhappy did not. You and your mate can maintain dedication to each other by keeping a positive vision for your future.

Contrast this with what chronically unhappy couples do. They nurture an obsession with the past rather than a vision for the future. And most of the time when they talk about the past, they talk about failures, conflicts, and disappointments. Sometimes you do need to talk about the past to better understand something that happened or to work through forgiveness. But regularly talking about wonderful times in the past will remind you that your marriage is much more than what might be happening right now. Don't let yourselves get focused on past disappointments. Focus on your future together.

Setting Goals

One very specific way to develop your vision together is to talk about your goals for the future. Do you know the adage "If you fail to plan, you plan to fail"? Most of us know goal setting is wise, but too few of us do very much of it in marriage. Solomon described planning ahead as the path to blessing (Proverbs 21:5), as true in marriage as in anything else.

It doesn't take an hour each evening to keep your future goals clear. I know couples who talk about goals in a structured way once a year. For example, Wendy and Glenn carve out a couple of hours every New Year's Day to talk about their goals for the year—what better day? Sure, there is plenty to do on that holiday, but they have found they can make the time. When they meet, they talk about goals for several major areas: spiritual, financial, relational (marriage), and children.

One year they agreed to spend thirty minutes, two days a week, to nourish their spiritual relationship, and also picked out devotional material to read to each other. Although they didn't keep to their plan perfectly, having it in place enabled them to find time together far more often than ever before.

They also talked about how they were doing financially and how much they wanted to save in the coming year. They didn't follow that plan perfectly, either, but having it helped them save more than they probably would have otherwise. In both cases they achieved goals that were reasonable and that stretched them beyond where they would have been. Decisions don't have to be applied so rigidly that they sap the life out of you.

Wendy and Glenn are not slaves to a formula, but they recognize that spending this time together is valuable. The actual goals they set are helpful to them, but talking about their future together is even more powerful. It reinforces the overall sense that they have a future and a vision for it.

Short-term goal setting is valuable too. When you plan and set goals for the week to come, you alleviate the pressures of conflicts that often arise during daily routines. The benefits of long-term goal setting, however, have more to do with enhancing and realizing your vision for the future. A solid vision that includes goals keeps you headed in the direction you want to go.

One caveat here. In marriage, as in much of life, clinging rigidly to goals when circumstances change is unwise. There are times for flexibility about the plans we make—strong couples rise to the occasion and move ahead through the trials of life. If you develop a routine for goal setting in your marriage and keep at it, one goal should be to reevaluate all goals based on any new circumstances.

Sharing Dreams

Like sharing goals, sharing dreams greatly benefits your marriage. It's one more way to demonstrate the reality of a future together. But dreams are different from goals, so you share them somewhat differently. Marriage goals are what you plan to accomplish together, whereas dreams in marriage are what you hope to experience together. Hence, dreams touch the deeper hopes of your heart.

Sharing dreams can be positive, but you won't do much sharing if your marriage is not going well or if you don't both have a strong sense of safety based on commitment. That's because dreams reveal more about who you are than goals do. As I said earlier, research my colleagues and I conducted at the University of Denver shows that couples with greater levels of dedication disclose more deeply in their marriages. An atmosphere of mutual dedication, along with a sense of a future, makes it safer to share dreams. And as is true of many aspects of commitment, this dynamic works in both directions. Sharing your dreams can reinforce an atmosphere of mutual dedication and having a future.

If you already share your dreams with your spouse, keep it up. It's healthy for your marriage. If you don't share dreams but would like to try, I encourage you to do it cautiously. Be careful to treat your mate's dreams as something precious, something that's coming from the deeper regions of his or her soul. If you stomp on your mate when he or she is sharing dreams, or demean the dreams that are shared, you'll seldom hear your mate's dreams again. Invalidation and conflict will shut down the pipeline through which the deeper connection flows.

For this reason, it can help for you to agree to share dreams and thoughts for the future in a certain way. I suggest setting aside time just for this purpose—you might want to take a walk together or go out to dinner—and agree to keep conflicts and issues off-limits. It's a powerful way to make a positive investment in your marriage.

Kim and Alex have made that kind of investment throughout the twenty-five years they've been married. While their children were at home, they spent a great deal of time as a family. They introduced their kids to new experiences, enjoyed traveling together close to home and in several other states, and encouraged their children to follow their interests and dreams. But Kim and Alex also made it a priority to spend quality time as a couple. They had regular dates to go to a movie or enjoy a quiet dinner together as friends. They also set aside time to discuss parenting issues and to work out problems when they disagreed. And, very important, they continually shared their hopes and dreams for the future.

For Kim, those dreams included having her own business. For years her passion had been designing and making innovative purses. She had started making them for herself and then her daughter, and soon a number of friends started asking her to make one for them. While the children were young, she was content with her part-time job and with giving her purses as gifts. But she always dreamed that some day she could turn her creativity into a full-time, exciting business.

Alex's dream was to travel to Europe. With the expenses of growing children and an older house, there had never been a lot of money for extensive vacations. But Alex had always hoped that someday he and Kim would have the time and money to travel in another part of the world, learning about other cultures.

Now that their children are grown, there is more of an opportunity for Kim and Alex to fulfill their dreams. But until they're actually able to, they are continuing to do what they've always done: share those dreams and encourage each other in reaching them. For example, when Alex is in a bookstore, he often looks for sewing and crafts magazines that might interest or inspire Kim. He's also given her books on how to set up your own business and asks her about her vision for creating a line of purses. On Kim's part, she encourages Alex to tell her about the places in Europe he'd like them to see. She also stays on the lookout for talks and slide shows about Europe that the local travel store often holds. When they find one that sounds exciting, they go to it together.

Kim and Alex have always talked about their hopes and dreams for the future. Their ability to share such personal things has been a great blessing. It has also produced many benefits. First, it's made each of them feel heard and validated, which has knit their hearts closer together. Second, it's allowed each of them to encourage the other—for example, Alex's buying inspiring books and magazines for Kim and Kim's looking out for talks that Alex would enjoy. Such thoughtfulness and encouragement remind both that they're cared about and loved.

Third, it gives them a sense of a future together. If they ever choose to turn their dreams into something they want to make happen, they can start making plans for reaching their goals. Sharing dreams brings blessings both for now and for later.

What do you dream about? What about your mate? Have the two of you shared your dreams? Knowing about your mate's dreams makes it more likely you'll be able to develop dreams for your life together. What do the two of you want to be doing together when you are sixty, seventy, or eighty? Do you see yourselves traveling? Baking? Exercising? Making love in the afternoons? Playing together with your grandchildren? Working together in a charity or ministry? Holding hands while swinging on a porch somewhere? Reading good books side by side and snuggling? You don't have to be clairvoyant to believe in a future. You do need to share your dreams and have a sense of a future together.

One more word on sharing dreams: if you have tried to share your dreams but have been put down, don't give up. Keep doing what you can to make your marriage safer for this kind of intimacy. For some of you, that means learning more about how to handle conflict well. For help in that area, please see *12 Hours to a Great Marriage* and other books I have cowritten with Howard Markman and other colleagues (see Resources).

Sharing Faith and Practice

One of the most powerful ways that couples can deepen their shared life vision is by learning to share their faith. Researchers have known for a long time that those who are more "religious" tend to do a bit better in marriage. Note that I'm saying a bit better—not overwhelmingly better but consistently better.[14] This means that there are many couples with clear and even strong faith who have poor marriages and many who have no faith yet have great marriages—at least by noneternal standards, such as happiness, security, and quality parenting.

So how does faith have an effect? When it is practiced together. Couples who have similar faith and beliefs *and* who practice their faith together do much better in marriage than couples from different faith backgrounds.[15] In a very well conceived and well conducted study, perhaps the best ever conducted on this topic, Annette Mahoney, Ken Pargament, and their colleagues at Bowling Green State University looked carefully at how faith affects marriage.[16] The researchers studied the degree to which partners shared the belief that marriage is sanctified—that is, the degree to which they believe that marriage, their marriage, is special to God; the degree to which couples believe that God is manifested in their own marriage; and the degree to which partners engaged in acts of faith as a couple, sharing the practice of their faith rather than merely being religious as individuals. What the researchers found was that these elements were strongly related to how couples' marriages were doing.

If you and your partner do not share a common faith, there are still things you can do to strengthen your marriage. My colleagues and I cover those things in some detail in other books (see Resources). For those who do share the same beliefs and faith, my question is simple: Have you considered how to deepen your walk of faith together? There are many ways to do this, and the reason to do it is not merely to strengthen your marriage—though it is one of the most powerful ways you can do exactly that. If you believe, you also are likely to believe that there is a larger meaning to life and to what your marriage is all about.

Consider some of the following possibilities, remembering that your way as a couple may be different from other couples' ways:

- Share your walk of faith.
- Share the impact of Scripture passages and other readings.
- Pray together.
- Listen to or sing hymns and spiritual songs.
- Worship together.
- Share a ministry together.
- Work together to help the downtrodden and disadvantaged.
- Perform meaningful rituals together.

Although there are many more ways to have a deeper, fuller, more meaningful union, my goal here is to plant a seed of what is possible in your marriage. How you pursue the possibilities is up to you and your spouse. But will you pursue them? Are you already doing so? Brainstorm together what is possible and what you are willing to try together. Taking small steps toward big goals can cause great things to happen.

KEY COMMITMENT ACTIONS

- What are your goals for the future? What are your spouse's goals? Talk together about short-term goals as well as what you would like to have accomplished five, ten, and twenty years from now. Set aside regular time to continue talking about goals and to update or adjust them as needed.
- What are your dreams for the future? Share them with your spouse, openly and honestly. Then ask your spouse to tell you his or her dreams. Listen with respect and acceptance.
- Think of several ways you can encourage your spouse in making at least one of his or her dreams come true. This can be through verbal support or by doing tangible things to help your spouse follow the dream.

Now add and take your own action steps to strengthen your commitment even more:

_____

_____

_____

Chapter 9

Grieving and Growing

O n the day we marry, most of us believe we are gaining a best friend for life—we are aware of gaining a lot on that special day. It would be far less typical to think about what we might be giving up. For example, when you married you probably committed yourself to forsake all others, but at that time you probably had no "others" in mind. So you didn't feel you were giving up much of anything.

But because there's so much of life ahead of you when you get married, it's nearly impossible to fully comprehend what you're forsaking when you say "I do." I'm not saying you can't make a full commitment on your wedding day; what I am saying is that you can't know all of what your commitment will mean in the years to come. Commitment does ask you to give up some things in life.

Even in a great marriage, you probably will be aware from time to time that your marriage is not *everything* you had hoped it would be. Maybe you've found that your marriage falls short of your dreams, or perhaps you've come face-to-face with an attractive alternative you won't pursue. When disappointments arise, you're likely to have a feeling of loss. This realization can hit like a blast of cold air that takes your breath away, or it can seem more like a slow leak, leaving you drained and flattened. Being committed hurts at times, and an occasional (or, for some, chronic) sense of loss is a fundamental element of commitment. Although some people seem deliriously happy together over many years, most people feel a sense of loss at times, even though they may not talk about it with anyone.

This chapter talks about dealing with feelings of loss in productive ways, ways that will honor your commitment and not tear apart your marriage.

Grieving the Loss of Your Dream

For one couple, the loss of their dreams about marriage came particularly hard. It was after midnight as Nicole paced up and down the hallway outside her bedroom. Her husband, Eric, and their two kids were fast asleep. Listening to the quiet, Nicole felt terribly alone. She felt sad, and had a sense of loss. She kept thinking, *How could Eric be so different now from when we met?* Those thoughts had been coming more frequently over the last few months. As she tried to think through exactly what was wrong, she realized, *It's not that I have a bad marriage; it's that I don't have what I wanted or expected.*

Although Nicole didn't know it yet, she was grieving the loss of a dream. She and Eric had met when they were both seniors in college. Dating had been a wonderful time of discovery for them, and those discoveries had included both similarities and differences.

Both had a similar faith. Both liked to be physically active—Nicole loved aerobics, and Eric was an avid runner. They did not have the same political views, but it was fun to explore the differences. Even when they disagreed, it was fun to talk things out. Over the year that they dated, they drew closer and felt completely compatible. When they realized they were in love, thoughts of marriage followed.

One thing that Nicole had especially loved about Eric was that he had plans for the future. She had plans, too, but it was particularly important to her that he knew where he wanted to go. Eric had planned on a career in public relations. He loved to write and plan, and he had figured that public relations would allow him to get paid for doing something he really enjoyed. Nicole had planned on a career in counseling. That had sounded great to Eric—he never felt more attracted to her than when they talked at length about something philosophical or theological. It had seemed like they could sit around and drink coffee and talk for days.

Now, twelve years later, things were quite different. Eric and Nicole had been married for eleven years and had two beautiful children—Taylor, who was eight, and Briana, five-and-a-half. Nicole and Eric felt good that they were providing a solid home for their children, and the kids were doing very well. But their marriage was not. Certainly Nicole and Eric were kind to each other and treated each other with respect. But neither was experiencing much joy in the marriage. The closeness and fun they had experienced while they dated was gone.

As Nicole paced and thought, she realized that with each passing year she had become more disillusioned with her marriage. She was happy with the work she was doing at a community mental health center, but Eric was not happy with his career. He had finished college with a degree in writing and public relations, but he'd never found a very good job in the field. Eleven years later, he was employed in the same job he had accepted right out of school: working in the public relations department of a company that made tires. Although Nicole appreciated that Eric held a steady job, it was relatively low-paid work that didn't offer him opportunities for advancement or intellectual stimulation. He had looked for other work for a while, but had finally given up the search. And he seemed to have given up on himself as well.

As Eric's despair grew, he became glued to the sports channel. The remote control seemed to be permanently attached to his hand. And though he watched sports all the time, his own interest in physical activity had disappeared. He no longer ran, and he'd gained weight from snacking in front of the television. He was increasingly passive and unmotivated. He had become someone to whom Nicole was not at all attracted.

Nicole still loved her husband, but she didn't like a lot about him at that point. She began to spend less and less time with him. Her feelings of loss and loneliness grew daily, but she was ashamed about how she felt and therefore reluctant to talk about her feelings with anyone. Then she had a realization—she was feeling the way she had felt when her father died. That puzzled her. *No one's dying here*, she thought. Then it came to her: *My dreams for this marriage are dying*. The thought scared her. "Until death do us part" seemed like a long, lonely time.

For his part, Eric had been aware for some time that his work was pulling him down, but it was much less painful to simply accept the situation. He hadn't been able to figure out how to make his job more interesting or meaningful, let alone find another one. He let time go by.

Yet despite his passivity, Eric was actually grieving over his marriage too. He and Nicole no longer talked the way they used to. When they did talk, it was always about money or problems with the kids. It was just too threatening to talk about the problems the two of them were having. It upset him. And as he continued to think about it, he began to believe that Nicole had deceived him while they were dating. After all, they no longer talked about politics or philosophy or anything at all deep anymore. Soon he became certain that she had deceived him, but he failed to notice that he had changed from the person Nicole had dated and fallen in love with.

What had started as a marriage with promise had become something quite painful. Neither Eric nor Nicole was happy with the person the other had become. But because both of them believed in sacrificial love, they remained stuck, not sticking. And both felt grief about what they had lost.

Commitment and Loss

As I plow into this sensitive theme, I want to make one thing very clear. I believe that generally people who live out their commitments end up with far richer lives and relationships for having done so. In other words, the gains of commitment far outweigh the losses that come from making—and sticking with—certain choices.

However, a discussion of commitment would not be complete without discussing those losses. Even if your marriage is almost perfect, what you want may change enough to cause you to feel a sense of loss. For some of you, that feeling of loss may be deep and chronic; for others it may not be much or frequent. Whenever you do feel a sense of loss in your marriage, however, it may seem too big or too tangled to work through productively. But you have three options for dealing with the misery:

- Change your expectations.
- Change the situation.
- Actively grieve the loss.

Although I will discuss the three choices separately, keep in mind that there are times when you'll end up engaging in all three. Real life does not come neatly packaged in separate categories. So I suggest you approach a sense of loss in this way: first, identify the expectation you have that is not being met. Second, determine if the expectation is reasonable or not. If it is reasonable, work toward changes in yourself and your marriage to bring it about (change the situation). If it's reasonable but not something that's likely to change, actively grieve its loss by following the model I describe later in the chapter. If the expectation is just not reasonable, then you need to change it within yourself. Otherwise, you will simply make yourself unhappy.

Managing Expectations

We all have expectations of life: expectations of our mates, our families, our work, and nearly everything else. Some expectations are very specific, but others are not; we are aware of some of our expectations, unaware of others. Although expectations are not the primary focus of this book, they are a significant topic with regard to grief and commitment. If you would like to further examine your expectations and learn how to handle them, I encourage you to pick up one of the many books available to help (see Resources).

In marriage, expectations affect everything. You probably have expectations about who will do what around the home, whose work outside the home is more crucial, how your children should be raised, ways you'll be physically intimate, how close you'll be, how you'll make decisions, and on and on. The losses you feel in your marriage come from the difference between what you expect and what you get. When you don't get what you expect for the most part, you feel sadness and grief, even if the expectation was unreasonable.

You need to think about important expectations and determine whether or not each of them is reasonable. It's also very important to talk with your mate about what you expect. One of the most unreasonable expectations of all is that your mate will know what you expect without your having to say anything.

Both Eric and Nicole grieved the loss of what had been a great part of their friendship—the ability to talk about a variety of interesting topics. Their expectation had been that they would continue to have great talks from time to time, and that expectation was completely reasonable. But they had let that kind of sharing slip away. (We'll look more at what they could do about this in the next section on changing the situation.)

Nicole also felt a sense of loss that Eric was far more passive than she had *expected* him to be. Her expectation might have been reasonable, but it also might not have been, because Eric might not be able to change much at this moment, or he might be unwilling to. If he's unable to change, Nicole needs to grieve over Eric's present passivity. But it's possible that he could change in the future. People do change. Although Nicole strongly suspects that Eric will always be more passive than she expected, she does not know that for certain.

If Nicole changes her expectation about Eric, her sense of loss will be lessened, and she will be less disappointed. But that's not the whole of it. Changing an expectation also involves grieving, because you are giving up something that was part of a vision. Sometimes, though, changing an expectation does not so directly involve grieving. For example, if you expected that your marriage would be free of conflict and now you find that it's not, you could conclude that your original expectation was unreasonable. You could grieve over that, but the expectation is likely to go away once you see how unrealistic it was. You can reorient your expectation in line with the realities of life.

? *Did You Know . . .*

In addition to conducting research on marriage at the University of Denver, I have worked with hundreds of couples in my office and in workshops. These people have told me what they long for, including the following:

- A more financially responsible mate
- A more emotionally sensitive mate
- A more athletic mate
- A more (or less) sexually responsive mate
- A mate who is more active as a parent
- A more musically sensitive mate
- A more physically attractive mate
- A more spiritually active or sensitive mate
- A mate who is a more effective housekeeper
- A mate who is a better listener
- A less emotionally volatile mate
- A more emotionally expressive mate
- A mate who shares specific interests
- A mate who shares more tasks around the home
- A mate who loves to go out on the town
- A mate who loves to stay at home
- A mate who is more protective
- A mate who is handier around the home
- A mate who makes more money
- A mate who works less (or more)
- A mate who is a soul mate

What about you? What do you desire that has not come about?

Changing the Situation

Before we delve into grieving, let's consider what you may be able to do, alone and with your spouse, to make changes when they seem possible.

Changing What You Do

Most of us look in the wrong place when we want to make a change in our marriage. I'll bet you've heard the story of the man out on the street late at night, bending over looking for something under the street lamp.

A stranger comes up, offers to help, and says, "What did you lose?"

The hunched-over man says, "I lost my car keys."

"Did you? Right in here somewhere?" the Good Samaritan asks.

The first man replies, "Why, no, I lost them over there, but the light is better here." Before looking for what's missing in your mate, which is usually like searching for a key in the wrong place, stand under the light and take a good look at yourself. There you are more likely to find the key you can turn to improve your marriage.

The most productive move you can make when you are not pleased with the way your marriage is going is to change yourself. Instead, most of us tend to want—even demand—change from our mate. After all, it's easy to dwell on how the other person is failing.

It's not always possible to have a relationship, especially marriage, the exact way you want it to be, even when what you want is good and right. You can't control the other people in your life. You can't make your mate into your ideal woman or man. You *can* make changes in the way you act and react. One spouse trying to force the other to be someone he or she is not succeeds at nothing but generating strife.

Let's go back to Nicole and Eric for a minute. Neither can make the other do much of anything. Nicole cannot drag Eric away from the television. She cannot make him be more active about his career. She cannot force him to take better care of himself physically. She can decide, though, to take better care of herself. It's possible that Eric would become more interested in physical fitness again if Nicole sets an example.

For his part, Eric cannot force Nicole to be interested again in having the kinds of talks they used to love. He can decide to start reading again, though. He can show both himself and his spouse that he is still interested in great books and talking about issues and ideas. It wouldn't be reasonable for him to expect Nicole to be interested in talking with him when she sees him interested only in watching television.

Changing What You Do Together

Eric and Nicole could change some things if they worked together. They could recapture the connection they experienced when talking about interesting topics; they are both still capable of having those kinds of talks. But making the change would involve one or the other daring to speak up, and that would mean taking a risk— admitting gently but openly that there was a deep desire for something that was not happening.

You can work together to change your marriage. If your mate is not the way you would like him or her to be, you can talk about it and work to see what can be done to make your marriage more mutually satisfying. It takes trust to have such a talk and teamwork to make the change happen.

Eric and Nicole are doing fairly well in some ways, but they do not have the sense of being a team. Each feels quite alone and has a sense of loss. Without feeling more connected, it will be difficult for them to make changes happen.

If either of them does want to try changing as a couple, he or she needs to go to the other and ask for help. This is best done with humility and gentleness, not with anger or in a demanding way. For example, Nicole could choose a quiet moment to say something like this to Eric: "I've been thinking about how things are going for us. I think we are far more distant from each other than is good for our marriage. I miss being close to you and wonder if you miss it too."

Or Eric could say, "Nicole, I've been thinking about how our life together is going. I think we've lost something we once had. We used to talk so much about things we were both interested in. I realize that I've been pretty distant for some time, and I'd like to try to change that. I'd like to see if we can get back on track."

Note the liberal use of the words "we" and "us" in these statements. Also note that no sense of blame or hostility is conveyed. That makes it possible for the person being addressed to respond positively and for the two partners to develop a sense of being a team, looking together at what can be done to rebuild their relationship.

Contrast those statements with the kind of accusatory statements that spouses all too commonly make:

> "Why can't you get off your behind and *do* something with your life?"
> "You're so lazy. Look at what's happening to your body. You have a beer gut, for goodness' sake."
> "You know, I used to think you were an interesting person to talk to. I was wrong. You're very boring."

You get the idea. Making such statements will not bring you closer to what you want. They amount to questioning the character of the person you're talking to. They also portray a pessimistic view of what's possible in the marriage. And they do not promote peace. People will not open up and want to work with their mate if they are on the receiving end of such comments.

In addition to speaking to each other sensitively, Nicole and Eric can do a lot to head their marriage in a better direction. Let's suppose they want to draw together to bring about changes. They can resume talking together about fun and interesting subjects—they'll need to make that a priority and set apart time to make it happen. They can also resume working out together. All kinds of good can come from feeling better physically. One of the really powerful things they can do together, given that they are both open to it, is to develop their spiritual life together.

Change may not be easy, and it won't happen overnight. But Nicole and Eric can do it. They've only misplaced, not lost, their ability to talk on a personal level and to share things that are important to them. They will find obstacles in their way. For one thing, they are far busier now than they used to be. Making time for conversation or working out together will be harder at this point in their lives—there are kids' schedules, work, household tasks, and the like that also require time—compared to when they were in college. But they can make the changes if they put their minds to it.

However, there may be one or more major problem areas that cannot really be changed. One might be Eric's passivity about his work situation. Of course, it could change, but let's assume that it's not likely to change at this point. Because having Eric be more proactive is important to Nicole, she is going to have to deal with the reality of the situation. She can examine why it's important to her. It might be that she sees their economic future as more dependent on

Eric than on her. Or it might be that she has trouble respecting someone who just lets life happen. After thinking about it, Nicole could decide that what she expects from Eric is not realistic. That may help some, but she will still need to grieve the loss.

Healthy Grieving

The word *grief* usually refers to painful feelings associated with the loss of someone or something that cannot be replaced no matter what we do. For example, most of us grieve when a loved one dies because we cannot reverse the loss. For the purposes of this book, I'm defining grieving as the active process of working through feelings of loss in ways that are consistent with one's integrity and commitments, and in ways that promote healing of the soul.

Perhaps you think you don't need to read this section because at this point you have no need to grieve the loss of anything in your marriage; if that's your situation, I'm happy that you haven't experienced loss. However, please read on, because some of the ideas may be helpful to you in the future.

Let's begin with what grieving is not.

Grief Versus Despair

Whereas grieving is a process of actively feeling and dealing with a loss, despair is the opposite—it is a passive process in which you feel a complete loss of hope. Despair is the end result of a growing sense of futility, the belief that nothing constructive can be done about the present situation. Grieving is something you actively engage in and learn from; it improves you. Despair grinds you down into hopelessness.

In marriage, a sense of despair most likely comes from a combination of three factors: (1) a sense that things are miserable; (2) a sense that things cannot change; and (3) a sense that the suffering involved is meaningless (in other words, that it is not good for anything, including spiritual growth).

Consider Eric's situation with his job. He has fallen into despair about it. He might not be clinically depressed, but he no longer thinks about what he might do to improve his work situation—he has given up.

Nicole is seriously affected by his despair; despair is infectious in marriage. If both Nicole and Eric fall into a long-term pattern of despair—about his work, about their lives, about their marriage— they will truly be stuck. Their marriage will grow colder and colder until all the life in it freezes up.

Becky and Matt experienced a terrible loss, but they didn't give into despair. Happily married for twenty-five years, Matt was a manager at a parcel delivery service, and Becky ran her own insurance business from their house. They had remained close friends and were involved in all kinds of activities. They had managed their money well, and with their children launched they were planning to buy a boat and spend weekends and vacations sailing off on many new adventures together.

On a Monday morning just like any other, Matt left for work. After Becky kissed him good-bye, she decided to run to the office supply store to pick up a few things she needed. She got into her car and merged onto the highway for the short trip to the shopping center. Then, as she rounded a bend, she looked across the median to see an eighteen-wheeler barreling toward her. There was no time to get out of its way. The huge truck, its brakes out, smashed into her car at fifty miles an hour.

Becky was so severely injured that Matt barely recognized her when the doctors finally allowed him to see her. She was badly bruised and swollen. Her pelvis, shoulder, and back were broken. She lay unconscious for days, Matt never leaving her side. When she finally awoke, she was told she would be in the hospital for up to three months and would need months of physical therapy following that.

A year after the accident, Becky and Matt's lives were still upside down. Becky had made excellent progress, but she was racked with chronic pain. Nothing she tried, neither conventional medicines nor a variety of alternatives, helped very much. The constant, tremendous pain limited her movement, affected her concentration, kept her from working, and made it hard for her to enjoy herself.

The losses began to pile up. Not only did Becky suffer, but Matt did as well. It was hard for him to see his wife in such pain, and he missed his life partner's enthusiasm and the things they had shared before the accident. They both missed just being "normal." This included making love, which was impossible because of Becky's constant pain.

Both Matt and Becky could have sunken into despair. But instead they talked openly about how the accident had changed their lives. They couldn't do the day-to-day things they had done. They wouldn't be able sail and do many of the other activities they had looked forward to. They had suffered an irreversible loss. They had to change their lives and their dreams.

Happily, the commitment Becky and Matt had made to each other remained strong and vibrant throughout their ordeal. There was no question in Matt's mind that he would stick with Becky despite the changes. He felt a terrible loss, but he did not feel stuck. Becky felt the same. So they fought for their marriage, hung together, grew closer, and did not give into despair.

When a loss like Matt and Becky's occurs, there is nothing to do but accept it. Becky and Matt did this while remaining committed to each other. But because their future was so affected by their loss, they also had to grieve for what they would never have.

They had to adjust their dreams, but they did not have to give up.

Life doesn't always turn out the way you expect it to, sometimes in dramatic ways. Committed couples hunker down and stay the course. Although they may experience pain, they may also know the great joy of overcoming challenges and loss together.

Exercising Your Commitment

As the writer of Proverbs (most likely Solomon) said, "Hope deferred makes the heart sick, but a desire fulfilled is a tree of life" (Proverbs 13:12 ESV). In that text, the Hebrew word for "hope" is *towcheleth*, which means "expectation." The Hebrew word for "sick," *chalah*, has the root meaning "rubbed" or "worn"—by implication "grieved," "pained," or "made sick." To put it simply, unmet or delayed expectations and longings grieve the heart. They rub at it; they wear it down. Can you think of a time in your marriage when something you longed for did not happen, and consequently you felt grief over the loss? How about something that you really wish were in your marriage but is not—not now and perhaps not ever? If the two of you know how to talk safely and deeply, talk about these things. Draw together in understanding and acceptance that you each are imperfect—but wholly loved.

Strategies for Grieving Productively

Most cultures don't grieve very well. In the United States, we try not to grieve at all by working hard not to incur any losses. Many people act as if they will get through their entire lives without suffering loss. They plan to accept only gain.

Of course, you can live only so long before something goes wrong and you can't change it, and you feel completely humbled. Everyone will eventually be humbled by death if by nothing else. So let's not pretend that we will never incur any losses. We will grieve at times, but grief can drive us closer to understanding wisdom in life.

To grieve productively, consider the following tips.

Accept the Feelings. If you are sad or upset about something you don't have in your marriage, it is better to deal directly with those feelings than to pretend they are not there. If you ignore such feelings, they may pop up at other times as either withdrawal and distancing or resentment and irritability. These behaviors will hurt your marriage. On the other hand, if you deal with your feelings of loss both honestly and openly, you can take control of them to some degree. You may not make them go away, but you will benefit rather than harm your marriage.

Accepting and dealing with feelings of loss does not mean dwelling on them. That could cause malaise and inaction. Instead, take action, meditating on the strength of your marriage and your mate and talking with a good friend about your loss.

Don't Blame Your Spouse for Being Who He or She Is. Part of productive grieving in marriage is accepting the loss, and part of accepting the loss includes accepting your mate for who he or she is. Remember the vow you took "to love and to cherish"? You need to keep working on loving and cherishing the one you married, and there is no more powerful way to do that than by showing acceptance. In the book *Fighting* for *Your Marriage*, my coauthors and I stressed that the desire for acceptance—and thus, the fear of rejection—is the root of much conflict in marriage.

It will do Nicole and Eric little good to continue being upset about who the other person is. There is no way one can know all about a mate before marriage. Further, people really do change over time. If your mate turns out not to be exactly who you thought he or she was when you said "I do," you have a choice. You can be resentful and punish him or her for not conforming to your dream, or you can become more accepting.

Please understand, however: you shouldn't accept wrongs or irresponsibility without challenging them. My intent here is not to recommend accepting outrageous or dangerous behavior from your mate. But unless you are in a destructive relationship, you can benefit by choosing to accept your mate more fully in many areas. This requires patience, contentment with what is, and an active commitment to forgive—to forgive your mate for who he or she is not, including any real sins as well as failures to live up to your dreams.

Grieve Together

This idea may seem a bit strange to you, but some couples have something that is an amazing picture of grace and commitment: they have marriages that are so strong, with such a level of trust, that the partners are able to talk openly together about grief and unmet expectations.

A colleague recently told me about one such couple with whom she was working. The couple shared their deep sense of loss for how their marriage was turning out. Each described things they had expected or dreamed about that were not happening and might never happen. My colleague talked candidly with them about grieving for and accepting their losses.

The couple immediately acted on my colleague's ideas. At the next session they told her how they had already incorporated the concept into their private language. For example, during the week when the husband had hoped he could talk with his wife about what was going on in his work, and she had not been able to listen without being critical of him, he closed up and pulled back a bit. After giving him some breathing room, she walked over and sat down beside him and said, "Grief?" He replied, "Yes, grief." That's powerful validation rooted in acceptance and forgiveness.

The couple fully understood that each was disappointing the other and that each felt grief. However, they had begun to convert their individual experiences of grief into a vehicle for drawing closer together. Doing so can affect a marriage so positively that it's hard to put into words. But it's only safe to do so if the commitment is clear.

The Power of Forgiveness

One of the obstacles to healthy grieving in marriage is an inability or unwillingness to forgive your partner—either for not being perfect or for ways he or she has hurt you. As you can imagine, you are not very likely to be able to grieve in the healthy way I'm promoting here if you are unable to forgive. But what is forgiveness?

I have asked Natalie Jenkins, who has coauthored other books with me, to write the following section on forgiveness. Forgiveness has been a major focus of all the books I and my colleagues have written to help couples prevent marital distress and divorce (see Resources). Among our team members, Natalie has taken the greatest interest in this subject over time, devouring all the recent research[1] and thinking about how to refine the points. So here is Natalie's advice on forgiveness. Following it I will make a few comments about what she said in the context of the main message of this chapter.

✂

The only person I know who married someone perfect is my husband. So the joke goes. But when we stop to think about it, we remember one of the truths we learned as kids: no one is perfect. That means that at some point everyone on the planet has been careless, irresponsible, mean, selfish, stubborn, uncaring, arrogant, jealous, or incorrect, and has not done what he or she should have or has done what he or she should not have. Everyone makes mistakes, and that means everyone has hurt and been hurt by others. Even those we love, perhaps especially those we love, will hurt us and be hurt by us at some point. This section addresses what to do when one spouse hurts the other.

Payback

When you're hurt, it's natural to want to seek revenge, to hurt the person who hurt you. To some there's a sense of needing to correct the moral scale. When one is wronged, the "rightness" of the world feels out of balance until the offender has been wronged in return. To others, the desire to hurt back comes from the need to teach the offender a lesson. The thinking is, "I'll teach you that you can't treat me like that."

Still others, when they've been hurt, assume it was because the offender believed they were unimportant. Thus the wounded may seek revenge as a way of proving that they are valuable and deserve better treatment.

All these reasons for revenge have a common theme. It's the idea that hurting someone in return will make the person doing the hurting feel better. The question is, Is it true? If one person has been hurt, is the world going to become a better place if two people get hurt? If you hurt someone, have you really taught that person to treat you better, or have you simply taught him or her that you have the capacity to cause pain? If you hurt someone because you believe it makes you important or valuable, does this truly make you more worthy of respect?

There's really nothing wrong with the *goals* behind a desire for revenge; it is OK to want to make things right again, it is OK to want others to learn to treat you well, and it is OK to assert that you are a valuable person. What isn't OK is the method that revenge requires. Inflicting injury of any sort on your mate isn't OK, and it won't get you closer to what you long for in life. Fortunately, there are more effective ways of making things right again.

Forgiveness: What It Is and What It Isn't

I define forgiveness as *giving up your perceived right to get even*. It is a strategy for making things right again that does not involve revenge. Before we talk more about what forgiveness is, it is important to understand what forgiveness is not.

Forgiveness is not forgetting. There is a common myth in our society that if you can still remember an offense, then that proves you haven't forgiven the offender. This is simply not true. If you have forgotten something, that is evidence of brain malfunction—nothing more, and of all the known causes of brain malfunction, forgiveness is not listed among them. The link between forgiveness and forgetting is not literal, but more figurative. It's the idea that once the offender has been forgiven, then the offended can move forward without the painful event permeating every conscious moment. The memory of the event begins to move from the present into the past.

A rabbi once told our team that a lack of forgiveness was, in his theological system, a kind of "remembering against another." It's not just that one remembers, but one remembers in a way that holds the other in a one-down position.

Forgiveness also is not pretending that unacceptable behavior is acceptable. Sometimes when someone has been hurt, you'll hear the person say, "Oh, that's OK." But forgiveness does not mean that the offended person is saying that what the other did was all right. When there is forgiveness and restoration, the offended person is saying, *Our relationship will move forward. I'm not going to hold this over you; I'm not going to choose revenge.* Unacceptable behavior needs to be identified and discussed, and the offender needs to be held accountable for his or her behavior.

Forgiveness is not "letting the other off the hook" or releasing the person from natural consequences. That point is made in the following story:

There was a man who was very distraught. He had decided a long time ago that life was not worth living and finally decided to do something about it. He took the elevator to the top of a very tall building. He went onto the roof. He walked to the edge and looked over. He stood there pondering. Finally he decided that his life truly was not worth living, and he wanted to end it. So he jumped. On his way down, he decided that he had made a mistake. He prayed, "Oh, God. I've made a mistake. Please forgive me." This happened to be one of those rare times in history when God spoke audibly. He said, "My son, you are forgiven. And by the way, I'll see you in a moment."

In our world, there are natural consequences just as there are natural laws. Gravity doesn't stop because you wish it might. When one hurts another, there are consequences even if there is healthy forgiveness. If one partner lies to the other, he or she may be forgiven, but trust will be lost, at least for a time. In the same way, if one spends more money than agreed on, he or she may be forgiven, but the money does not magically appear back in the bank account. If one partner has physically abused the other, he or she may be forgiven, but the victim may no longer trust the other. These are examples in which forgiveness and reconciliation may be different. You can forgive another by giving up the desire to get even, but it may not be wise for you to reconcile the relationship. Reconciliation often depends on the degree to which the one who has done something wrong—or a series of things wrong—takes responsibility and makes amends. Which brings us to trust.

Forgiveness is very different from trust. Trust is a function of trustworthiness and is earned by repeatedly demonstrating trustworthiness. The offended person chooses to take risks by trusting the offender in direct proportion to the evidence the offender has provided. Forgiveness is not based on the behavior of the offender. Forgiveness is based on the value the victim places on freeing himself or herself and others from the tyranny of retribution. Choosing to forgive is choosing to release both parties from the chains of bitterness and the compulsion to hurt another.

Finally, forgiveness is not the same as grieving. When you forgive, you choose a path on which to walk, but it does not mean you will automatically reach your ultimate destination. Eventually healing is possible—healing is the goal. Forgiveness is the path and grief is the desert through which that path travels. One can forgive but still experience grief and pain from the wound.

In contrast to forgiveness, revenge is often based on a belief that hurting someone back would make you feel better. Is it true? For some, there seems to be a temporary feeling of satisfaction. Anger can make us feel strong. Seeing another hurting at our hands can make us feel powerful and self-righteous. But this happens at a cost. Hurting another person diminishes the self. It hardens the heart and destroys friendship, trust, a sense of safety, and intimacy. Will you feel better in the long run if you hurt your mate or if forgive your mate?

The subject of forgiveness often comes up when we think about major infractions and hurts in life, and it is as relevant in marriage as it is anywhere else. No marriage and no mate is perfect. Forgiveness is crucial in marriage because you cannot move on to healthy grieving for losses in your marriage if you actively harbor bitterness and resentment that keep your mate in a one-down position for life. Forgive and seek mutual acceptance if you want your marriage to be a truly great one.

✧

If you are willing to accept loss and grief as important life lessons, very good things can come from them. That might sound trite, but it can be powerfully true.

Loss humbles you. Loss reminds you that you are *not* in control of everything. A time of loss is often the most powerful time for change, because everything that does not matter is stripped away. Healthy grief can lead to great things in your life and in your marriage.

KEY COMMITMENT ACTIONS

- Consider whether any feelings of frustration or sadness you have might be the result of unmet expectations. Try to pinpoint those expectations and think about whether or not they're reasonable. If you are greatly affected by unmet expectations, talk about them with a counselor or read in detail about handling unmet expectations (see Resources).
- If you discover you have a reasonable expectation that is not being met, work on making changes in yourself or in your marriage that will lessen your disappointment and feeling of loss.
- Has your partner ever done something that you've been unable to forgive? Keep in mind that forgiveness is not forgetting and that unless you forgive your mate, your partnership won't be as strong because your partner will be in a one-down position. Work on accepting that the hurt was done and moving on together.

Now add and take your own action steps to strengthen your commitment even more:

_____

_____

_____

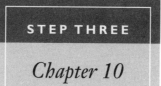

Chapter 10

Investing for the Long Haul

D uring the late 1920s, more people than ever before were investing their savings in the stock market. Until that time, most people in the stock market were speculators, meaning that they had a short-term view of their investments and were going for quick profits. They were looking for an immediate killing, not steady, long-term growth.

A popular speculative strategy at that time (one that's still popular) was to buy on margin. When you buy on margin, you don't have to have all the money to pay for the stock you're buying. You put up only a percentage of what the stock really costs; in a sense, you take out a loan from the stockbroker for the rest. People invested this way through the 1920s, and because the market kept going up, the investments didn't seem very risky. Life was good.

In 1929, however, as economies across the world started to decline, the market started to come down too—way down. Soon it became an out-of-control train careening down the mountain. People who were used to the good times and to quick gains were shocked—people who "want it now and want it quick" often don't tolerate loss very well. Investors began to sell out in droves and few wanted to buy, which brought prices tumbling down. Those who had not bought on margin did poorly. Those who *had* bought on margin were totally wiped out. They lost the money they had and a lot of money they had essentially borrowed but didn't really have. They fell, with no net to catch them.

Imagine you were one of those investors. You jumped into the market because all your friends were doing it and because it seemed a quick way to make some bucks. You bought a lot of stock—far more than you could really afford—using a margin account with your broker. Then you saw the prices of your stocks plummet. Your broker called and said, "You are losing a lot of money on your investment, and we're calling you in to make up the difference." You didn't have the difference. So you lost all your financial assets, and you dissolved into cold panic and nausea.

Many couples also think about their marriage in the short term instead of the long term. They focus on immediate returns, not on good value. Part of really sticking and not getting stuck is learning to be a wise investor in your marriage. Let's evaluate the kind of wealth that matters most in marriage; then we'll look at how to invest to build it up.

Relationship Capital

A definition of *capital* is "wealth that is used to produce more wealth." The term is usually used in connection with money or other business assets that help the business grow.

But people have different kinds of assets. Some folks are rich in money. Others are rich in relationships. If you've been wise, you have built up *relationship capital.*[1] *Relationship capital is what comes from investing emotional and spiritual resources in key relationships.* In marriage, relationship capital is your reservoir of resources, including positive bonds, trust, confidence, support, and spiritual connection—the sense of being in this together and being able to count on each other. This capital is a priceless treasure.

Many problems in marriages come from mistaking material gain for true wealth. You cannot buy relationship capital with money. The theme in the song "Can't Buy Me Love" hit home for the Beatles, but Solomon was on to the theme quite a bit earlier:

> Many waters cannot quench love,
> neither can floods drown it.
> If a man offered for love
> all the wealth of his house,
> he would be utterly despised.
> Song of Solomon 8:7 ESV

Time and energy count most at home. Those who invest the most in their marriage are those most likely to have a long-term, satisfying marriage. And those who have long-term marriages are also the most likely to end up with the greatest financial security.[2] Divorce wastes resources, and the failure to invest wisely in the marriage relationship contributes to divorce. In many ways, the deeper riches of a strong relationship and the blessings of financial security are most likely to come to people who are actively committed to their marriage over the long term.

When you invest wisely in your marriage, you also build relationship capital that can take you through tougher times. Have you ever seen married friends go through a horrendous situation, such as the loss of a child or the diagnosis of cancer? Perhaps you've dealt with such things firsthand. When faced with such a crisis, some couples fall apart, but others draw closer together. Those who come together are the ones who have built up some capital in their marriage; they have something to draw on. Couples who have not built up capital or who have squandered it have no reserve. When the tidal wave hits, they are washed away and the marriage drowns.

How do you invest and build capital? Let's look first at how you do it with money and then apply some financial principles to marriage.

Marriage and the Stock Market

I am not a financial adviser, but I know what you are likely to hear if you go to a financial adviser and say this: "I would like to save for retirement. Where should I put most of my savings?" Unless retirement is virtually upon you, you'll likely hear that you should put a great deal of what you can invest in the stock market. Why? Because in the United States, the stock market has been the single best place to make long-term investments over the past half-century—on average, nothing else has come close. Of course, investing in stocks is somewhat like taking a roller-coaster ride, which is what makes it seem so risky.

I believe there are some telling similarities between marriage and the stock market. Marriage is a great long-term investment. Satisfaction in marriage, however, goes up and down all the time, kind of like the Dow-Jones average, a major indicator of how the market is doing. Some stocks undergo fewer bumps and dips than others. Some days and months see fewer ups and downs.

The same goes for marriage. The "happiness rating" in some

marriages is more volatile than in others. Some couples' satisfaction level bounces around a lot more than others. But long-term commitment will carry you through the ups and downs of married life. You are not guaranteed that your investment will yield the return you are hoping for. Some people have suffered significant losses in their marriages. But, by far, most who consistently invest in their marriages will do very well over the long term.

Couples with a short-term view of marriage often do the same things that people with a short-term view do in the stock market. They try to time things. They move their investment in and out, trying to get the best deal over the short run. They cash in when it's all going downhill and try to buy back in when life looks better. Like short-termers in the market, they look for immediate gain, closely watch the score, and move their investments around based on how each day is going. Short-term investors tend to buy and sell at the wrong times, losing a little or a lot in each transaction.

Those with a long-term view of marriage behave differently. First, they don't pay excessive attention to the short-term dips. The long-termers don't react very much to the downs because they expect them. It's part of the long view. As a financial publication stated: "Investing for long-term prosperity is fundamentally different from trying to win at the short-term game. Indeed, Wall Street's measures for forecasting near-term results can be useless compasses for an investor whose horizon is ten years off. But it is the long view that will have the greatest impact on your worth. Now more than ever, investing for the long haul means screening out extraneous noise."[3]

The long-term view helps you react less to the "noise" of day-to-day life. It limits your risk because it steadies your investing. Only the future will tell if the accepted financial wisdom of today holds true in the decades to come. But I am certain that those who will do best in marriage—no matter what happens with the economy—are those who approach marriage as a long-term investment.

Long-term investors tend to invest even more when the market goes down. Why? Because they know they get even more stock for their money. A down market is one of the best times to invest, but only if you have the long-term view of investing. When your marriage hits a slump, it's a great time to invest more.

Investing in your relationship is the most powerful way to tell your mate that you're here and that you're committed to him or her and to your team. If you keep investing over the long term, you'll usually see a favorable result.

Did You Know . . .

When you are fully committed and you act on that commitment in your marriage, you will not only develop the attitudes of a good investor but also develop trust. When you trust, you place your confidence in someone who has been there for you. You trust because you've seen that person come through for you time and time again.

In marriage, trusting means having confidence in your mate's commitment, actions, and follow-through. Trust is a fundamental type of relationship capital you can build. When you have trust to bank on, you are more able to make it through the low points. You have confidence that you'll keep moving forward together and not get stuck in the present. Trust also makes it safe to keep investing, even when things don't feel quite right. Just as trust grows slowly in the first place, it is rebuilt very slowly over time when something bad has happened to deplete it.

> You also can't make your spouse trust you. However, you can consistently show yourself to be trustworthy by acting on your dedication and investing in the relationship. You can also grow in your trust for your mate by taking risks. Try making some investments and watch what happens. If your investment produces good results, you'll gain more trust. That is how you build it.

Relationship Capital and Trust

Nancy and I have had our blowouts over the years. I suspect very few married couples get through life without having some. But I trust her and her instincts deeply. That trust came from observing the way she handles decisions and priorities over many years.

Once Nancy confronted me in a way that highlights the intersection between trust and the long-term view of commitment. I had been in yet another period of working too much. Nancy thought I was looking particularly ragged (departing, no doubt, from my natural good looks and youthfulness!), and she was concerned. (I want to point out here that she would have had no good reason to be concerned if she hadn't been in love with me and committed to me. She was and she is. And I love her and am committed to her.) Anyway, she found me in front of my computer one day, working, of course, and took the opportunity to voice her concern. She said, and I quote, "You have to slow down because I'm the one who's going to be changing your diapers when you are old."

Sometimes I don't hear Nancy's concerns as well as I should. Although the way she expressed it was unusual, that time I got it right and didn't become defensive. One of the reasons for that is that she said what she said gently. I cannot tell you strongly enough how important that is when you confront your mate about something. Research confirms how crucial a gentle approach is at such times.[4]

Another reason I didn't get defensive was that Nancy and I have built up trust. We don't have a perfect marriage, but we do have relationship capital to draw on. When she confronted me, her gentleness, combined with my trust in her, helped me hear what was most important. Here's what I heard: "Dear, I love you, and I'm going to be here for you all the way—until you or I fall apart—but I'm worried about how much you work. I'll be here for you when you're old and gray, but I want you to leave something for me!"

That's a long-term view of love. Nancy made a deposit that day in our bank of relationship capital.

Investing for Growth in Your Marriage

If you are married, you are probably aware of ways the two of you have invested together in money and material goods. But there are less tangible investments to make with your time, effort, talent, and self-disclosure. Even telling your mate how you like the toothpaste tube squeezed is an investment. Making some of these investments involves a real expenditure of effort over many years.

When things are going well, either you won't think a lot about all that's been invested in the past or you'll think of it with settled satisfaction. When things are not going well, you're more likely to think about what you have invested in the context of what you might lose by leaving. That's a constraint, as discussed in Chapter One. But what you invest now is determined more by your dedication than by constraint. *You invest more time and effort when you are dedicated. Dedication based on the long-term view moves you to put more effort into your marriage today.*

Taking the Risk

Just about any kind of investment carries some risk. In life, you cannot control everything. You can't make it all turn out for the good. It's possible that even though you do your best, you have married someone who does not try to keep the marriage strong, and you feel lonely and distant. That's the scary part. *You can put in a lot of effort and get nothing back.*

I often hear that concern. When it's based mostly on score-keeping and shortsightedness, it needs to be dealt with as a poor attitude that harms marriage. But sometimes this fear is based on a realistic appraisal of one's mate.

Nonetheless, your marriage has the best chance of doing really well when you choose to invest yourself in it. Choosing not to invest guarantees that your marriage will get stuck or stop altogether. No matter what your partner does, you can make investments.

My father-in-law has passed on from Alzheimer's disease. He was a farmer, and my mother-in-law is a retired schoolteacher. Like many couples, they went through tough financial times, but they always kept saving. You cannot be a farmer without understanding how uncertain the future can be and how you need to keep investing and saving.

During the past several decades, my wise in-laws plowed much of their savings into the stock market. They weren't the kind of people you would think of as risk takers. They were very careful, but they came to understand something that many people never do: it's riskier *not* to invest than to invest and risk something. On the day after the stock market experienced the largest one-day decline in recent decades, they made another sizable investment. That's taking the long-term view. That's acting on commitment.

Stocks and other long-term investments have some risk, but all of life is that way. If you don't invest, and just consume all your resources today, you will surely lose in the future. Solomon understood this point very well, and he expressed it in this image of farming I made use of in Chapter One: "He who observes the wind will not sow, and he who regards the clouds will not reap" (Ecclesiastes 11:4 ESV).

People who always watch out for what might go wrong and don't take any risk often end up with nothing. I called this wind watching earlier on. Waffling and perpetual hesitation do not build a grand life. If you want to reap good things in your marriage, you have to take some risks. If you go through your married life thinking *I won't take any risks; I don't want to suffer loss or pain*, you will surely suffer loss or pain. If you really want to build relationship capital in your marriage and family, take the long-term view on what you are doing and keep investing, no matter what. That's a central part of what it means to be truly committed to your mate.

Being Disciplined in Your Investing

Most people who develop true wealth (in any sense of the word) have a strategy. They understand the long-term view and make commitments based on it, and they invest *regularly*. If you talk to a financial adviser about how to do well in the stock market over time, he or she is likely to tell you about a strategy called dollar cost averaging, or DCA. With DCA, you decide how much you are going to invest in the market and invest that amount in regular intervals, whether the market is up or down, soaring or crashing. *You invest no matter what.*

This strategy keeps you from reacting to the state of the market. It is a rational approach only if you believe that the stock market is fundamentally a good long-term investment. As I said, I think marriage is such an investment. It works out well only with a solid long-term view. Having a long-term view and a plan to accompany it keeps you from bailing out during short-term dips and losing what you invested.

What does DCA look like in marriage? Only you know the best investments for your marriage, but some of the more potent investments for many marriages are listed here. Any of them could add to your relationship capital over time. But remember that each of them requires time. If you do not carve out time for them, you can't make the investment, and you won't reap the benefit. Nothing will happen without the investment of time.

- Talking like friends
- Doing something fun together
- Leaving small notes of appreciation
- Planning a special date (together or as a surprise for your partner)
- Working on a budget together
- Expressing your love in some new way
- Resolving a conflict about money as a team
- Taking a walk together
- Planning a vacation together
- Going to church, synagogue, or other spiritual services together (worshiping together, praying together, engaging in a ministry together, and the like)

Exercise Your Commitment

What investments do you and your spouse make in your marriage? Spend some time talking about the things that matter most and that help the two of you stay close. Make a list of those things that are of the highest importance to your mate, that touch his or her soul; make another of those that are of the highest importance to you. You may discover that there are significant things that one of you didn't know about the other. Too often we invest in things that mean a lot to *us* but that aren't as important to our mate or that don't tell our mate that we know who he or she is.

Once you understand the kinds of investments that will bring you closer, make them a priority. If you would like help in thinking through how to most strongly convey love and investment to your mate, I highly recommend Gary Chapman's book *The Five Love Languages*.

I once cleaned the spiders out of all the window wells in our home because Nancy really wanted me to. I must admit I didn't do it right when she asked, which would have been more impressive to her. Nevertheless, I did it, and Nancy was pleased. That might not seem like much, but such little acts are investments in a marriage. Share what matters to each of you. Then regularly work at investing the time to make them happen. Wise investors stay at it, even when the conditions don't look right. Regular, steady investing profits a marriage. As Solomon said,

In the morning sow your seed, and at evening withhold not your hand, for you do not know which will prosper, this or that, or whether both alike will be good [Ecclesiastes 11:6 ESV].

Keep sowing seeds in the field of your marriage. I'm not talking about sowing wild oats here, but sowing the best of yourself, which will bring the greatest blessings back to you. You don't always know which investments will turn out best, but as Solomon points out in the passage here, when you keep investing, the harvest will be plentiful.

Investing in a Variety of Connections

I know some of you are thinking now, *But what about diversification?* Thought you had me, didn't you? Yes, financial professionals say it's important to diversify. It's important in marriage, too, but you don't diversify by multiplying spouses. To be sure, some people hedge their bets by being married while keeping a competing relationship going on the side. But clearly that's not good for marriage. So what is?

Diversify in ways that will keep you and your spouse connected. You can develop a close bond in your spiritual lives. You can make your sexual relationship more fulfilling. You can engage in fun activities together. You can do things together that benefit your children, which will often tie the two of you more closely together. See where I'm going with this? Most couples probably can't have every connection rolling smoothly all the time—some things go better than others at different times. But the more avenues of connection you have up and running, the stronger your marriage will be. That's diversification.

Many couples I have seen have only a sexual connection. Now don't get me wrong—a physical connection can keep couples close on a number of levels. But such couples are not diversified. When sexual complications come up—for example, after a baby has just arrived—the marriage will take a huge nosedive. During the latter stages of pregnancy and right after a baby is born can be stressful times for couples anyway,[5] but if the couple is connected only sexually, weakening that connection will spell trouble. Couples who regularly invest in a variety of connections will be less vulnerable to setbacks in any one area.

In the work I have done with my colleagues on how couples can preserve and protect their marriage over time, I have come to believe that the most powerful investment they can make is to *stay connected in their marriage as friends* and to protect their friendship time from conflict.[6] Staying connected in this way is crucial for building relationship capital. Over the years, too many couples stop making time for their relationship the way they did early on. When life gets busy and demands on time grow, friendship time usually gets sacrificed. That reflects short-term thinking. You need to maintain your friendship for your marriage to make it in the long term. Whether you invest in two-hour dates or twenty-minute walks around the block, you need to be together as friends on a regular basis.

But keep in mind what friendship means. Friendship involves talking about things that are enjoyable—not just problems and difficulties, but topics that draw you and your spouse closer. Married couples who aren't investing in friendship devote most of their talking time to problems. Although of course it's important to have these conversations and handle them well, it's also important to talk as friends. So make time for friendship to happen, and agree to keep conflicts and problems off-limits. Instead, talk about interesting topics: dreams, fun, philosophical issues, beliefs, experiences, spiritual impressions, prayer requests—you get the idea. Doing this will give you time to relax away from the pressures of life. It's a powerful way to deepen and preserve the bond you have over many years to come.

Following Rituals and Traditions

Rituals get a bad rap. The term is associated with stilted, overly regulated behaviors that have lost whatever power and meaning they once had. Many marriages and families derive closer connection and a sense of identity from rituals and traditions that are repeated throughout their lives. Such traditions anchor people in the past while helping them look to the future.[7]

One ritual that couples can benefit from is taking a yearly vacation to the same place. This may be boring to some people, but for many families it's a powerful tradition that supports their sense of family. For instance, many people I know who live on the East Coast went to the shore every summer with their families. For them, it was part of what summer with family meant. For you it could be going to the same lake or mountain for a day or a week year after year. The important thing is that you practice your ritual, whatever it is, as a couple and as a family. Rituals and traditions cement the sense that "we are a family," "we do things together," and "we have a future together." Simple day-to-day actions, taken over and over, can have a powerful effect.

To add to your list of rituals, consider the following:

- Walk together after dinner, talking about things friends talk about.
- Go to sporting events together and root for "the team."
- Give a present on each of the twelve days of Christmas.
- Plan a yearly weekend getaway to a romantic setting—just you and your spouse.
- Have a special meal on certain holidays. Prepare it together.
- Pray together about major goals on New Year's Day.

Exercising Your Commitment

Traditions and rituals are important both to our marriages and to our family lives. With your mate, make a list of things you do on a regular basis that are important to both of you and that reinforce your sense of being a couple or a family. Talk about other traditions you'd like to begin, and start incorporating them into your lives.

The Mystery of Oneness

Although many people these days believe that marriage causes pain and misery, marriages that are founded on full commitment provide some of the richest rewards possible in life. But great marriages are built over time, not created in an instant. They are like multi-course dinners, with varying dishes, flavors, and stages, not an instant meal heated up in a microwave.

But just because you have a future together does not mean you are building a great marriage. Without a firm foundation, it makes little sense to build anything. Are you building something or just expecting a lot from the concrete? You need to build by making regular investments in your marriage and your mate.

If your marriage is really thriving, you'll build something not quite like any other marriage around. Sure, it will be similar on the basics, including commitment, respect, and hope. But it will be different because it will contain what you and your spouse bring to it. This is important. Great marriages have a special kind of oneness, a oneness in which the two partners combine in some mysterious way to make a third, highly prized identity, "us." This kind of oneness is inherently mysterious. And as I said earlier, it has nothing to do with one person's identity being lost in the other's.

Why do I emphasize the idea of mystery? Because it means that a great marriage can't be reduced to a simple formula. The positive side of connection in marriage, and all the things you and your spouse need to do to build and maintain that connection, are part of the mystery of oneness. Couples whose marriages are coming apart tend to fall into one of two categories: either they have regular, nasty conflicts or they have a growing coldness and distance. The nasty-conflict couples tend to look like others who have nasty conflicts, and those who are growing apart tend to look like other couples who are growing apart. Yet the positive side is so much different. Different couples have different kinds of positive connections than other couples have. Couples who have a great marriage can look completely different from other couples who also have a great marriage.[8] That's the mysterious side of oneness.

So think creatively about what matters most to the two of you. Pursue a deeper understanding of the kinds of investments you make that touch your mate most. Although they may be different from the investments other couples make, if the two of you both regularly invest in your marriage in a lively, creative way, you will build the kind of mysterious oneness that your heart longs for—like that of Adam and Eve, to be *naked and unashamed.*

⁂

Unless you are going on to the next chapter, the optional chapter for those of you who are really struggling in your marriage, this is where I leave you. I hope you have found encouragement and new ideas that you can and will use in your life. The really great news about commitment of the sort we've studied here is that there are many things you can do to deepen it.

But remember that commitment requires action. You can't just sit back and reflect on it or wish you had it. Acting purposefully on your commitment from deep within your heart will accomplish the most in your marriage. That's I *do*, not *maybe* I do, and that is the power of commitment.

 KEY COMMITMENT ACTIONS

- Are you making regular investments in your marriage? Is your mate? Think about some of the things you do—big and small—that are building up relationship capital. Think about things your mate does that are doing the same.
- Set aside time to talk with your spouse about the investments you're making in your relationship. Ask your spouse to tell you which investment of yours is the one he or she appreciates most, and do the same for your spouse. Then talk about things you both can do to increase the investments you're making.
- Think of ways you can increase and diversify the connections between you and your spouse. For example, if you feel that your friendship connection is strong but your physical connection could be more fulfilling, discuss with your spouse what you both can do to make this happen. Work on strengthening as many of your connections as possible so that if one is momentarily lessened, the others will carry you through.

Now add and take your own action steps to strengthen your commitment even more:

_____

_____

_____

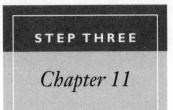

For Couples Who Have Lost Their Way

This chapter is especially for couples who have lost their way and are struggling, trying hard to decide if they have a future, or a future that will include any joy. I've included the chapter because I realize that although many couples who read this book are doing fine and looking for ways to build a good thing and keep it going, many are very unhappy in their marriage and may be thinking seriously about getting out. Please read this chapter if you are struggling but

- Your marriage is not dangerous to anyone in the family.
- You still have a flicker of hope, no matter how diminished and faint, that you can turn things around.

If you have already left your marriage, if your mate has left you, or if one of you has filed for divorce, it may be too late. Sometimes people don't see that things need to change until their mate has checked out of the marriage. And although the situation can turn around even after one partner has filed for divorce, I don't want to give false encouragement if there is really no hope. Likewise, if you've been a danger to your mate and she or he has left you because of that, the only path you should take right now is to get intense help for the problems that underlie that danger.

If your marriage is limping along but you want to give rededication a try, the best way to start is to determine that you really want to turn it around. One person alone can do a lot. In fact, you can effectively put many of the ideas here to work even if your mate doesn't know you are reading this book or trying to make things better. However, if it's open to you, the best path is for the two of you to work hard to move in a different direction and begin a better life together.

Making an About-Face

One of the greatest pleasures of my life has been to work extensively with chaplains in the various branches of the United States military. They are a hardworking, dedicated bunch of people who are on the front lines helping service men and women with their marriages and families. A navy chaplain I've known for seven years told me the following story of a turning point in his marriage (I've changed all names), and I'd like to use it to illustrate how change can be fueled by sacrifice and commitment.

At the time this happened, Dave and Melissa had been married for six years. Like many couples, they were struggling with various problems, and often they failed to handle their conflicts very well.

They would become upset, arguments would escalate, and he would often pull away. If it's not obvious to you, let me tell you that military life is very hard on families. They move frequently. In addition, service men and women have to travel a lot, sometimes to places where there is imminent personal danger. Schedules are not accommodating to the needs of family. Basically, military life can be high stress with low pay and a ton of duties to fulfill. It's easy for your spouse and your marriage to end up somewhere low on the priority list.

But Dave was not only in the military on active duty; he was also a chaplain in a full-time ministry. If being in the military is not hard enough on a family, think about being in a ministry! Pastors are pulled and tugged in all sorts of directions, many of which take them away from important matters at home. Pastors' wives also experience difficulty. Their roles usually aren't all that well defined, but they often include many responsibilities, and people served by the pastor expect much of them.

People who serve in ministries tend to be very responsible and have a hard time letting others down. But, like most of us, they have a tendency to presume upon the commitment of their mate, letting the needs of their mate slide when they're pulled in many directions outside the home. That's what happened to Dave and Melissa. Because both of them were talented people, others were naturally interested in availing themselves of their talents. And that made for some problems and some intense arguments at home.

Finally, Melissa leveled with Dave. Here's how the conversation went:

MELISSA: I hate you. I just don't know if I love you anymore. But I am committed to you.

DAVE: *(She had gotten his attention, and he was stunned.)* Are you saying you want a divorce?

MELISSA: You didn't listen to me. I said, "I hate you. I just don't know if I love you anymore. But I am committed to you."

DAVE: *(still reeling inside and not tracking very well)* What are you saying? Are you going to leave me?

MELISSA: Try again. I said, "I hate you. I just don't know if I love you anymore. But I am committed to you."

The third time, Dave finally heard what Melissa was saying, and he realized that he had an avenue of hope—Melissa's commitment. She surely was not happy, but the fact that she was keeping her commitment to him was clear. It might well have been easier for her to leave, but commitment called her to a tougher choice, to hang in there with him and attempt to change things. Score big points for Melissa's sacrificial spirit—it allowed her to confront Dave as well as make it plain she was sticking.

When Dave recalled their talk, he said that at that point he realized that years of erosion had damaged the positive bond in their marriage. Nasty arguments, misplaced priorities, and lost opportunities had taken a very heavy toll. He saw that Melissa was tired of driving on the toll road and wanted to find another road—but she still wanted to travel on the road with Dave.

Melissa's statement of pain and commitment led Dave to a conclusion, which he shared with me:

> I knew I had done a lot to damage the relationship by engaging in what I now know as destructive communication, which eroded the bond of friendship and any endearment (I guess you'd say low dedication). I knew that I had dug a deep hole and that it would take some time to get out of it. However, since Melissa said she was committed, I knew I could trust in that and work from there. It took about five years to rebuild and

restore our relationship. Yes, we did have some good times during that time, and with each passing month it got better. But you and I both know that without Melissa's commitment (not just constraint) to make the marriage work, I would be in a second marriage, and life would be so different.

Dave had the courage to invest in changing things with Melissa because he knew he could trust in her commitment to be there. Without the sense of permanence that comes from a clear commitment, who would put a massive effort into marriage? Sacrifice is hard enough as it is, but when there is no sense of a future, it seems purposeless and will be all the harder to accomplish. People don't invest if they don't believe that what they are investing in matters or that their investment will have the time needed to make a difference.

Melissa voiced her unhappiness, but she didn't threaten the commitment. Dave was moved by that. So he began to act in positive ways. After their talk, he took a three-hour walk dedicated to soul searching. When he got home, he committed himself to do two things. First, he decided to immerse himself in the book of Proverbs and to soak up its practical wisdom on relationships. Second, he decided to take the risk of asking Melissa for detailed feedback about what he was or was not doing that was causing her so much distress. That took guts. That was a sacrifice. That was courage matching the courage Melissa showed in confronting him.

A few nights later, Dave sat down with Melissa and asked her what she was upset about. He told her he would just listen and not interrupt or debate her concerns. He expected she would raise a few specific issues. But she began listing them and continued for some time. Dave ended up filling an entire eight-by-fourteen-inch piece of paper with the things he did that pushed Melissa away. He was humbled by it. Such humility is the root of real change in relationships.

Once Melissa finished her list, she and Dave made up new ground rules for dealing with their issues. From that day forward, they worked on their marriage in a different way. First they addressed the more fragile and volatile issues in their marriage. And they committed themselves to change and to teamwork.

Dave is still in the military and still a chaplain. There are still pressures on both him and Melissa. They don't always get along well, but they are a team. And because of their efforts together they have received the blessings that stem from working through the tough spots of life and coming out closer. Commitment kept them hanging in there—there was no *maybe* that things would work out.

Working on Your Marriage Without Your Mate

When it comes to marriage, I think I have heard it all, but I don't know your situation or your mate. I do know that some people who read this book will be led to deeper levels of pain and grief about their marriage than they have ever felt before, because the examples and concepts will make them think of elements they dearly wish they had in their marriage but don't. If you're in that situation, I want to encourage you that you can make things better.

I also want to encourage you if you are feeling stuck but are married to someone who will not try in any way to help you build your marriage. Perhaps your mate doesn't care or doesn't believe that anything more is possible in your marriage than what currently exists. I cannot tell you what you should do. I do believe that one person in a marriage can act on many suggestions in this book, and in doing so give his or her marriage the best possible chance. Very often, good things are eventually, if not rapidly, reciprocated in a marriage. It may or may not be true for you, but it's worth a valiant effort.

I would like to warn you about one thing if your mate is not going to help you. I've heard my friend and fellow researcher Howard Markman say this to couples in workshops for years. Even if you don't think that your mate is doing his or her part, that's no excuse for you to behave badly. You can't allow your judgments of your mate's failings to justify your own poor conduct. Tit-for-tat negativity destroys marriages. It does nothing in the effort toward sticking.

If you are in pain about your marriage, at least at times, I want you to know you have my empathy and the empathy of many others you're not likely to meet. I hope it helps you to know that. It's tough to try to stick when so much in life says to just stop. I hope you find the wisdom to know how you should walk. Go slowly. Think carefully.

? Did You Know . . .

One of the myths that affect marriages is that if you are down, you are out—that there is no coming back from an unhappy place in marriage. It is true that there are many damaged marriages that do not ever return to happiness. However, there are other marriages in which the couples do improve things or at least stick it out until better times. Perseverance does sometimes pay off. We looked at this point earlier, and it is worth looking at again.

One large household phone survey conducted by a research team of which I was a part asked over two thousand respondents many questions about marriage and divorce.[1] One question asked married people if they had ever thought their marriage was in serious trouble at some point in the past. As I've mentioned elsewhere in this book, 34 percent said yes, they had thought of divorcing their spouse. Of those respondents, 92 percent said that they were glad they were still together. That's a big number.

It is important to realize that marriages can change and that many people who stuck it out when times were very rough were later glad they did. Your marriage can be turned around if you are dedicated to making it different.

Sailing the Marital Seas

Recently I read one of Patrick O'Brian's books in his *Master and Commander* series. These are wonderful historical novels set in the days of sailing ships and the war between England and France. I have always liked books about oceans, ships, and war, and O'Brian's are done very well. They always surprise me with the depth of storytelling they offer along with the excitement they extend as they describe strategies and naval battles.

I've often thought of how similar marriage is to taking a prolonged ocean journey. Because some people are highly motivated by word pictures, I'm going to say a few things here about sailing ships from the Napoleonic era in order to make some points about marital commitment.

Bailing and Pumping

I never really thought about this before, but it's not surprising to find that many ships of the 1800s leaked terribly. Even those that leaked only a little would occasionally take on water when they encountered a storm or incurred some kind of damage. So ships' hands had to regularly pump out water. But that didn't mean that a ship was doomed if it had water coming in all the time. Leaks only meant doom if no one was regularly dealing with keeping the ship afloat.

Your marital ship is the same. No matter how nice a ship you have or how smooth your seas, you are going to take on water at some point. Taking on a bit is normal; taking on a lot is not. If you are taking on so much water that it seems you are bailing or pumping all the time, perhaps you need to pull into dry dock and fix some of the big leaks. To do that you need to find some supersticky stuff and plug up the holes. You might even need to see an expert to help you figure out what work needs to be done.

Bailing is not fun, but it is necessary. In marriage, you bail water when you work through a problem with your spouse or when you talk together well about something that is sensitive. Bailing takes work, and it works best if you do it together and regularly.

Exercising Your Commitment

In some of the other materials I've written with colleagues, we've talked about a number of strategies couples can use to solve problems together. One of the most important of these is to have regular meetings as a couple just to deal with the problems and issues in your lives.[2] Set aside time and create an atmosphere of respect and acceptance. Then discuss the issue until both you and your spouse understand it and both of you feel understood. Then work on solving the problem by setting an agenda for continuing to work on the problem, brainstorming as many potential solutions as possible, agreeing on one solution, and following through on what you decide to do. If the problem continues, adjust your solution to see if that works it out.

> Regularly working on your issues takes discipline and commitment, but doing it—together—can make your ship sail much more smoothly.

Although it's not bad or strange to take on some water, it is dangerous to let water build up. You likely have let a lot of water build up if you are part of a couple that is really struggling. So your task at this point is not only to get your ship back in sailing shape but also to learn how to keep it that way in the future. You need to plan on bailing but not bailing out.

Drifting in a Dead Calm

Imagine you are out at sea, sailing along nicely. Then, one day, you can't find the slightest breeze. That's OK for a day. But what if it's the same the next day, and the next, and . . . you get the point. Patrick O'Brian talks about this situation in his novels: the boredom, the frustration, and the danger if supplies start to run out.

Marriages can sail into dead calm seas. You stop making progress, there is no wind at your back, and you don't go anywhere. And it seems that there's not a lot you can do about it.

But is there something you can do? For one thing, you can tend to the parts of the ship that have been neglected while you've been racing through life. You can scrape barnacles so that your hull is smoother and ready to move when you do have wind. You can mend torn sails. You can polish the deck or clean out the areas below. You can also take some time to clarify your heading for when the wind returns to your sails.

My point is this: if you are not moving through the water as easily as you thought you might, your marriage is not necessarily in trouble. The wind will come back. Use the quiet time to do some things that will allow you to sail more smoothly when the wind returns.

Rowing

One option that sailing ships had when they were stuck in a dead calm sea was to put out all the launches and tie ropes from the little boats to the ship. Then the crew would start literally pulling for all they were worth to get the ship to a better place and pick up some wind.

Rowing is not nearly as much fun as sailing. But being very committed and learning to sail together do not mean you'll always have great wind. When there is no breeze in your marriage, you will sometimes have to put your back into it and row. And when you row, you move slowly. You have to expend more effort. You sweat. You ache. But you do keep moving. Rowing is a duty and a chore, and does not make you feel exhilarated. But because you have sailed before, you're aware that your ship is capable of more—rowing is only what you have to do right now.

If your marriage is pretty damaged at this point, it may be damaged not because you never had any wind but because you never knew to row during the times when you didn't have wind. In marriage, problems come up from time to time that take the wind out of your sails. You may have no idea why it has happened or when the wind will come back. At these times, you may not even feel like being on the ship with your spouse, but rowing is the only answer if you don't want to stay dead in the water. To move your ship forward when there is no wind will take all of your strength and the hard work of commitment.

Rowing can take many forms. When you work together to get through a tough problem, you're rowing. When you reach out together to seek advice from good friends about a struggle you are having, you're rowing. When you take the time to learn how to communicate more effectively or learn new problem-solving skills, you're rowing. When you read a book on budgeting and work toward a budget you and your spouse can live with, you're rowing. When you pray for blessings for your mate, despite being annoyed or angry with him or her, you're taking some big strokes of faith to get your ship moving again. All of this work comes from dedication and helps you build even greater dedication.

When you have the wind with you, fill your sails and let your ship roll on across the sea. Enjoy the view. When there is no wind, row and keep rowing. And whether you're sailing or rowing, don't lose sight of where you're headed.

Regaining Dedication When Only Constraints Define Your Commitment

In Chapter One I talked about two types of commitment that are both very important to success in marriage: dedication and constraints. However, constraints provide only a kind of security, not the fullness of love and devotion that dedication brings. If you have reached a point where you feel stuck in your marriage, it's most likely because you have lost touch with the fervor and rewards of dedication.

What follows is a plan for getting back in touch with that fervor and dedication. It's less a formula than a map—a map that can take you and your spouse back to the main road of your devotion to one another. Although there are likely to be a number of paths that you could take to the main road, I really do not think there is one any more direct than this one.

I will first share the essence of the map and then demonstrate the wisdom of this ancient way with two key illustrations from the Scriptures. The first is from the books of Ezra and Nehemiah in the Old Testament, in the story of the Jewish exiles' return from captivity. The second is from the Book of Revelation in the New Testament, in which Jesus challenges the churchgoers at Ephesus to regain their first love. I use these passages to bring out the power of the map for rebuilding your marriage. If you are religiously inclined, they may well touch you deeply. If you are not, I hope they will simply help you more fully understand the key points about regaining what has been lost. These illustrations highlight the steps on the path I am outlining for you.

The Map to Rededication

This plan is best followed by you and your mate together, though I have no doubt that it can be very useful to you alone if your spouse is at least open to having the marriage improve. Follow the map by moving sequentially through the three points. Move with all your strength toward Point A, then toward Point B, and, finally, toward Point C.

> Point A: *Remember* what things used to be like and what you had.
> Point B: *Resolve* to reverse course—to get back what you had, and more.
> Point C: *Restore* the actions of dedication.

How does the map work? When you remember the early days of loving devotion, you bring back some of the feelings you had then, and that can be powerful. Don't get me wrong: I think that the decisions of the will are far more important than feelings for regaining lost dedication, but those feelings can help you reawaken your desire to be closer to the person you married.

When you move through Point A, don't hurry. You will have more strength and energy for getting to Points B and C if you take your time working through Point A. And do not allow yourself to rewrite history. That's easy to do when you are unhappy in your marriage, because often your current feelings cloud your ability to see clearly the passion and excitement you once felt being together. Push by those filters. Look at pictures, think about special times, ask friends and family about their memories; do whatever you need to do to see into your past clearly enough to be touched in your core. Sometimes having memory is just as important as having vision.

Once you've spent time at Point A, you can move to Point B, and Point B doesn't require lingering as much as making a decision to press on to Point C. There you want to make a clear decision of the will—your will—to turn in the other direction, back to a better marriage. You not only have to want it, you have to decide it's going to happen—at least insofar as it depends on you. Make the decision and write it down. Also make reminders of the fact that you have pledged to move forcefully ahead to regain what was lost.

If you are working on this map with your spouse, mark your Point B decision with some kind of ceremony. This could be as simple as looking into each other's eyes and promising that you will each give the decision your best. Or you could take part in a church, synagogue, or marriage retreat recommitment ceremony. I would not wait for one of those for making the decision together, but if one is coming up, and you have already made the decision, it's a great way to make your stop at Point B very clear to both of you.

To move to Point C and then continue down the main road you seek, you must act on full and lively dedication. After you make your decision to act, you need to act on your commitment in ways you once did, and likely more. That means doing much of what the rest of this book describes, because that is what commitment involves.

As you work to rebuild your dedication and trust, remember that neither of you is perfect—not your partner, not you. Let your awareness of your own failings lead you to be gracious toward your mate's imperfect efforts to show his or her commitment to you.

Going Back to Jerusalem

I am now going to use this story of Jewish exile as a means of highlighting the points in this chapter.

The Jewish people had been taken captive by the Assyrians and exiled in stages and groups to Babylon. Assyria was eventually overthrown by Persia under the leadership of Cyrus, who allowed the Jews to return to Jerusalem about seventy years after they were taken into captivity. The return of the Jews to their homeland occurred under the leadership of Ezra and Nehemiah. (I encourage you to read the entirety of these two books of the Bible, as they are very rich in meaning.)

Two changes resulted from the Jews' return to Jerusalem. First, they rebuilt their temple—but not without opposition and delay. Second, they rebuilt the walls around the city under the leadership of Nehemiah. The first rebuilding is told in the Book of Ezra; the second is told in the Book of Nehemiah. However, there is great similarity between them because both deal with these central elements that are needed to recapture something lost:

- A remembrance of what was and a desire to return to it
- A decision to return and to do something about the desire
- A sustained effort to rebuild despite long odds and opposition
- Reinvestment in the habits of devotion

Both stories indicate that there was a rebuilding of the Jewish people's hearts that culminated in acts of connection with and rededication to their relationship with God.

How do these stories relate to restoring a marriage that has lost its way? First, unless you and your mate reclaim your dedication to one another, you are in a type of captivity. It may not be all that destructive—and as I've suggested in a number of places throughout this book, marriage offers benefits even when it is not thriving within full commitment. Yet it's captivity of a sort because you feel as though you are trapped, and, most important, you do not feel at home. Babylon may be pretty nice, but your heart wants to be in Jerusalem.

If you are stuck in captivity, it may seem easier not to remember what was lost—not to think about Jerusalem and the temple—but remembering is a powerful way to reignite the fire to return home. In your marriage, that is what you need to do, and that's what you do when you pass through Point A. Point A is about getting back in touch with your desire to be naked and unashamed with your mate.

The Jewish people in captivity wanted to rebuild their temple. This desire reflected the core of what they were deeply moved to do. Rebuilding the walls was important, but it was the temple that reflected their inner desire for restoration and wholeness. In a marriage that needs to turn around, you too need to start change from the deepest desire of the heart.

The resolve of the Jewish people to return to what they once had, especially in their relationship with God, is reflected in many ways in these stories. Here are a few verses from Nehemiah that reflect their movement from Point A to Point B on the map:

And they said to me, "The remnant there in the province who had survived the exile is in great trouble and shame. The wall of Jerusalem is broken down, and its gates are destroyed by fire." As soon as I heard these words I sat down and wept and mourned for days, and I continued fasting and praying before the God of heaven [Nehemiah 1:3–4 ESV].

Nehemiah is deeply grieved about what was lost, and his mourning reflects his strong desire to return to Jerusalem. His desire is so strong, in fact, that he risks everything—including death—to speak of it to King Cyrus (chapter 2 of Nehemiah). His feelings about Jerusalem move him to resolve to return there.

But in addition to focusing on acting on feelings, the stories in Ezra and Nehemiah are also about building a wall. Much about commitment can be symbolized in building a wall. Walls set apart what is within from what is without. Marriage says that within its walls lies a city of two.

There's more, of course. Walls protect. Walls guard what is kept within from the dangers outside. Nehemiah understood that the city could not be defended without walls. So did the enemies of the Jewish people and of Jerusalem.

In marriage, part of the job of restoring dedication is rebuilding the wall around the two partners. Although the wall may have been damaged in a variety of ways, it needs to be restored to provide the healthy boundary that gives couples freedom and makes them safe.

The three steps of the return to dedication can be seen again and again in the stories recorded in Ezra and Nehemiah. They are very evident in the culmination of the story cycle, the celebration of the Feast of Tabernacles. In that story, the Jewish people *remember* the history of their relationship with God, *resolve to return* to following Him, and set up various ways to begin to *restore their dedication*, such as by making various offerings (see Nehemiah, chapters 8 through 10). These are the core themes of restoration. No matter what the relationship, remembering, resolving, and restoring are the pathway to regaining the wonderful connection that has been lost. Marriage is no exception.

An Amazing Letter Points the Way

Let's look now at one other teaching about how restoration works, this one from the New Testament. You don't have to be of the Christian faith to have heard of the Book of Revelation. It's one of those books in the Bible that is intensely focused on the future. In Revelation, there is a sequence in which, in a vision, Jesus tells John to write and send letters to seven churches and have each letter address a particular concern and provide specific advice on how to improve. The letter to the Church at Ephesus is the one I find most amazing.[3]

> To the angel of the church in Ephesus write: "The words of him who holds the seven stars in his right hand, who walks among the seven golden lamp stands.
>
> "I know your works, your toil and your patient endurance, and how you cannot bear with those who are evil, but have tested those who call themselves apostles and are not, and found them to be false. I know you are enduring patiently and bearing up for my name's sake, and you have not grown weary. But I have this against you, that you have abandoned the love you had at first. *Remember* therefore from where you have fallen;

repent, and *do* the works you did at first. If not, I will come to you and remove your lamp stand from its place, unless you repent" [Revelation 2:1–5 ESV, italics added].

Remember, repent, do. Do these words seem familiar? Remember, resolve, restore. Point A to Point B to Point C. Note that in the letter the recommendation is not to spend time trying to figure out how the people had left their first love. The recommendation is based far less on insight than on action.

Although this letter is a message from Jesus to a church, you can see how the principles are very clearly applicable to a relationship—like yours—in which you need to regain your lost love. (By the way, the word used for love in this passage is the Greek word *agape*, which is understood to mean committed love. It is just like the concept I call dedication.)

Let's think more now about the advice the letter offered for regaining dedication. The first step is to remember, and remembering means to exercise your memory. What happens when you remember the early days of a loving devotion now lost? I don't know about you, but I start to feel things I felt back then. I can remember the feeling of excitement, the passion, and the sense of being alive. Remembering reawakens your appetite for what has been lost.

The next thing to do to regain loving dedication is to repent. There are many complicated ways to think about what that means, but it's not a complicated concept. It means to change your mind and head in the other direction—turn 180 degrees. If you are going in a direction you now consider the wrong one, then you turn around if you are wise. This plan is simple, but simple can still be hard. It takes some humility to decide to change directions in your life, and that may be the hardest part about it.

The last instruction here is simply to "do." Do what? Do the first things. Do the things you used to do. In marriage, that means you act on the kind of commitment that used to fuel so many good things between you and your partner. Make time. Share. Be kind. Sacrifice in all the small, meaningful ways that tell your spouse of your love.

Turning It Around

Remember Lisa and Steven from Chapter One? Lisa had been quite anxious on her wedding day, wondering if she and Steven had what it would take to make their marriage last. Seventeen years later, Lisa and Steven had a child, Kyle, age twelve. Lisa was working in a department store as a buyer of women's clothes. She worked hard, but she enjoyed it. Steven ran a small store that sold musical instruments. Music had always been something special for him, and his work allowed him to stay involved with musicians and music.

Lisa and Steven had a good work life. But Lisa's initial fears about her marriage had become reality over the years. Her marriage to Steven was stable, but both she and Steven thought they would probably be happier with someone else. Neither wanted a divorce because there were too many constraints. He worried that if they divorced he would not see Kyle enough, and he also didn't see how splitting up could be workable financially. He just didn't make enough on his own. Lisa had thought about divorce, but she was concerned about Kyle and about what others would think.

Lisa believed strongly in commitment in marriage, and she did not see how divorce could be an option. She thought there were only a very limited number of circumstances in which divorce would be acceptable, and the one she was living in was not among them. So she and Steven plodded on.

Lisa and Steven were stuck. Their marriage had once been a thing of real delight and beauty, like vibrant fresh-cut flowers. However, like flowers that are not kept in water, their marriage had become dry and brittle, and the petals had been dropping one by one. Seventeen years earlier, Lisa had worried about whether or not they would make it. Her anxiety had revolved around divorce. Now, although she and Steven weren't heading for divorce, they were off the road and in the ditch. Lisa thought this was not much better.

She and Steven were becoming more and more concerned about the direction of their marriage. But neither had much of an idea about what to do. Then, during a relatively rare tender moment, Steven simply said to Lisa that he missed what they used to have. His words touched Lisa, and she responded warmly that she felt the loss too. Steven said to her, "Let's do something about this."

What they did was go to a marriage enrichment workshop. The speakers covered such topics as how to communicate better and how to clarify expectations. Both Steven and Lisa brightened at what was said about preserving—for them, rebuilding—friendship in marriage, as both were feeling the loss of that very strongly.

Near the end of the workshop, a speaker talked about commitment and discussed the three powerful steps from the map we just studied. Steven and Lisa had not yet fully worked from Point A to Point B to Point C, but they had, on their own, taken some steps toward all three.

As they listened to the speaker, both Lisa and Steven felt something stir deep inside. Each had already thought of a few special memories from early in their marriage. Steven remembered a time they had gone hiking in the mountains together, got stuck out in a storm, then found their way back to their cabin, drenched and cold. They had built a fire in more ways than one. Lisa had thought about all the times they used to go to a special pizza parlor, relaxing over their favorite pizza, listening to music, and talking about anything and everything. They began to think of other great times.

The point about changing direction also hit home. With feelings tugging at both their hearts, Steven reached over for Lisa's hand. It was a small gesture that represented a deeper turning. Lisa's hand met Steven's with a strength he had not felt in years. Holding Steven's hand also reminded Lisa of something from their past—how they used to hold hands whenever they were together. It felt good back then, and it felt good again.

Steven and Lisa left the workshop encouraged that there were many things they could do to restore their relationship. They were reassured that they could do the kind of things that had once built a strong bond between them.

Getting It Done—Together

The next thing Steven and Lisa did was the hardest part of all. When they returned home, they talked about what they were thinking, and they did it without blaming each other. They talked and they talked. Then they talked some more. Both shared the sense of pain and distance they had been feeling. They even shared that they had been thinking that maybe their marriage could never be any more than what it was. They shared that they were hungry to have a real relationship; they wanted to regain what they had once had and go farther. They made a commitment to do it together.

Next, they made a plan of action. They planned time to talk about the past—not about the hurts and failings, mind you, but about what had been special. Steven talked about the passion. Lisa talked about the friendship. Both were encouraged to remember they had liked being close.

People can decide at any time that they are going to go in another direction and make changes. Even one mate's decision to change the marriage can move mountains. It's most powerful, though, when two people who are stuck decide together to get out of the ditch. That's what Lisa and Steven did. They hugged, they talked, and they committed themselves to do whatever it took to redevelop loving devotion, or dedication.

Lisa and Steven spent a couple of hours later in the week discussing all the things they used to do together that they could start to do again. Taking walks together. Taking a picnic lunch to the park. Going out to dinner and talking about whatever seemed interesting that day. Watching a funny movie together. Watching a romantic movie together. Sending Kyle to Grandma's for a night or two and camping out in the bedroom. They thought of many fun things that had drawn them together but that they had stopped doing years before. "No wonder the life got sucked out of our marriage," Steven observed. "We weren't doing any of the things that used to really draw us together." "I know," replied Lisa, "we let a lot slip away, and we were paying the price."

Lisa and Steven also discussed other things that they had let slip. Early on they had been more polite, more willing to make time for each other, more concerned about what would please the other, more attentive to the other's feelings, and more open to talking out problems as a team. They rededicated themselves to being kinder and gentler with each other in the rush of life. That's a fundamental part of acceptance on the day-to-day level.

Is this story a fairy tale? No. Lisa and Steven will have to keep working to maintain a vibrant, committed marriage. The press and strains of life too easily cause people to lose track of what matters most. Yet the path to rededication is not too hard to understand—

but you have to want to walk it and then move on. The directions are simple, but the work can be hard. I wish you all the best in making the journey.

 ### KEY COMMITMENT ACTIONS

- Assuming there is no danger in your relationship, determine with your partner that you both want to turn things around.
- At a time you've set aside for talking, voice your sadness about the current state of your marriage, without blaming your mate. Ask for feedback. Ask your spouse to do the same.
- Work through the three points on the map we talked about in this chapter: remember what things used to be like, resolve to get back to what you had, and restore actions of dedication.

Now add and take your own action steps to strengthen your commitment even more:

_____

_____

_____

• PONDERABLES •

Certain lines in this book are my personal favorites because they say so much with so few words—which, by the way, is an art and a gift that those who know me well say I do not generally have. I am listing here the most powerful of these one-liners for those of you who want to ponder more fully what they mean for your life.

- Commitment is making a choice to give up other choices.
- In marriage, the fences that go up around the relationship because of commitment allow barriers within the relationship to be pulled down.
- Yes takes too much time. (This briefest of statements comes, of course, from my son, Luke.)
- If you can number your days you can accept that they are limited, and then you can accept the need to prioritize, because there is not enough time to do it all.
- When you are very attracted to grass that looks greener, you can decide to move farther away from the fence. Hanging around a fence makes it easier to see the lawn next door.
- These days too many people want all the most enjoyable parts of relationships without any of the "hassles" of commitment, dependency, and responsibility.
- The problem with scorekeeping is its fundamental bias in favor of the scorekeeper, which from your perspective is you. If you do a lot of scorekeeping, you are sure to score many more points than your mate.
- Life almost never turns out well when you give up options before making a clear choice.

- You and your mate can maintain dedication to each other by keeping a positive vision of your future. Contrast this with what chronically unhappy couples do: they nurture an obsession with the past, rather than a vision for the future.
- Waffling and perpetual hesitation do not build a grand life.
- The most productive move you can make when you are not pleased with the way your marriage is going is to change yourself.
- Great marriages are built over time, not created in an instant. They are like multiple-course dinners, with varying dishes, flavors, and stages—not an instant meal heated up in a microwave.
- Remember that commitment requires action. You can't just sit back and reflect on it or wish you had it. Acting purposefully on your commitment from deep within your heart will accomplish the most in your marriage. That's I *do*, not *maybe* I do, and that is the power of commitment.

• NOTES •

INTRODUCTION

1. Waite, L., and Gallagher, M. *The Case for Marriage.* New York: Doubleday, 2000.

CHAPTER ONE

1. U.S. Bureau of the Census. *Marriage, Divorce, and Remarriage in the 1990s.* Current Population Reports, P23-180. Washington, D.C.: U.S. Government Printing Office, 1992. For current trends and statistics, I highly recommend the website of the National Marriage Project at Rutgers University (http://marriage.rutgers.edu).

   People often misunderstand what the "divorce rate" means. There are actually many divorce rates, depending on what you are studying. If you are interested in more information on this topic, see http://www.prepinc.com/main/docs/what_really_div_rate.html.

2. Amato, P. R., and DeBoer, D. "The Transmission of Divorce Across Generations: Relationship Skills or Commitment to Marriage?" *Journal of Marriage and Family*, 2001, *63*, 1038–1051; Amato, P. R., and Rogers, S. J. "Do Attitudes Toward Divorce Affect Marital Quality?" *Journal of Family Issues*, 1999, *20*(1), 69–86.

3. Stanley, S. M., Markman, H. J., and Whitton, S. "Communication, Conflict, and Commitment: Insights on the Foundations of Relationship Success from a National Survey." *Family Process*, 2002, *41*(4), 659–675; Scott Stanley, testimony on healthy marriage before the Committee on Finance, Subcommittee on Social

Security and Family Policy, U.S. Senate, Washington, D.C., May 5, 2004.

4. Reported in Whitehead, B. D., and Popenoe, D. *The State of Our Unions: The Social Health of Marriage in America.* Piscataway, N.J.: National Marriage Project, 2002; see http://marriage.rutgers.edu/Publications/SOOU/SOOU2002.pdf.

5. Whitehead, B. D., and Popenoe, D. *Changes in Teen Attitudes Toward Marriage, Cohabitation and Children: 1975–1995.* Piscataway, N.J.: National Marriage Project, 1999.

6. Popenoe, D., and Whitehead, B. D. "Who Wants to Marry a Soul Mate?" In D. Popenoe and B. D. Whitehead (eds.), *The State of Our Unions: The Social Health of Marriage in America* (pp. 6–16). Piscataway, N.J.: National Marriage Project, 2002; see http://marriage.rutgers.edu.

7. It is not at all true that couples in which partners have different faith backgrounds are doomed, but it is true that interfaith marriages are tougher and generally at greater risk. Younger people in general have no awareness of this, and they are also prone to think that it doesn't matter. It often matters a lot more to people when they have children.

These data are reported in a number of places, and can be found in Popenoe, D., and Whitehead, B. D. "Who Wants to Marry a Soul Mate?" In D. Popenoe and B. D. Whitehead (eds.), *The State of Our Unions: The Social Health of Marriage in America.* Piscataway, N.J.: National Marriage Project, 2002; see http://marriage.rutgers.edu.

See also Heaton, T. B., and Pratt, E. L. "The Effects of Religious Homogamy on Marital Satisfaction and Stability." *Journal of Family Issues,* 1990, *11,* 191–207.

8. See, for example, U.S. Census data as of the mid-1990s, reported in Bachu, A. *Trends in Marital Status of U.S. Women at First Birth:*

1930 to 1994. Washington, D.C.: U.S. Bureau of the Census, 1998; see

http://www.census.gov/population/www/documentation/twps0020/twps0020.html#abstract.

9. University of Michigan data cited in Whitehead, B. D., and Popenoe, D. *Changes in Teen Attitudes Toward Marriage, Cohabitation and Children: 1975–1995.* Piscataway, N.J.: National Marriage Project, 1999.

10. See, for example, Ahituv, A., and Lerman, R. *Job Stability, Earning, Marital Stability: How Are They Related?* Paper presented at the National Poverty Center Conference on Marriage and Family Formation Among Low-Income Couples, Washington, D.C., Sept. 2003; Nock, S. L. "A Comparison of Marriages and Cohabiting Relationships." *Journal of Family Issues,* 1995, *16,* 53–76; Whitton, S. W., Stanley, S. M., and Markman, H. J. "Sacrifice in Romantic Relationships: An Exploration of Relevant Research and Theory." In A. L. Vangelisti, H. T. Reis, and M. A. Fitzpatrick (eds.), *Stability and Change in Relationships.* New York: Cambridge University Press, 2002.

11. Johnson, M. P. "Commitment: A Conceptual Structure and Empirical Application. *Sociological Quarterly,* 1973, *14,* 395–406; Johnson, M. P., Caughlin, J. P., and Huston, T. L. "The Tripartite Nature of Marital Commitment: Personal, Moral, and Structural Reasons to Stay Married." *Journal of Marriage and Family,* 1999, *61,* 160–177.

12. This is a finding from many studies, including the following: Clements, M. L., Stanley, S. M., and Markman, H. J. "Before They Said 'I Do': Discriminating Among Marital Outcomes over Thirteen Years Based on Premarital Data." *Journal of Marriage and Family,* 2004, *66,* 613–626; Markman, H. J., and Hahlweg, K. "The Prediction and Prevention of Marital Distress: An

International Perspective." *Clinical Psychology Review*, 1993, *13*,
29–43; Gottman, J. M. "A Theory of Marital Dissolution and
Stability." *Journal of Family Psychology*, 1993, 7, 57–75.

13. These are some of the key publications related to commitment and
are based on the growing research in the field: Jones, W., and
Adams, J. *Handbook of Interpersonal Commitment and Relationship
Stability*. New York: Plenum, 1999; Johnson, M. P., Caughlin, J. P.,
and Huston, T. L. "The Tripartite Nature of Marital
Commitment: Personal, Moral, and Structural Reasons to Stay
Married." *Journal of Marriage and Family*, 1999, *61*, 160–177;
Rusbult, C. E., and Buunk, B. P. "Commitment Processes in Close
Relationships: An Interdependence Analysis." *Journal of Social and
Personal Relationships*, 1993, *10*, 175–204; Stanley, S. M., and
Markman, H. J. "Assessing Commitment in Personal
Relationships." *Journal of Marriage and Family*, 1992, *54*, 595–608.

CHAPTER TWO

1. Gardner, T. A. *Sacred Sex: A Spiritual Celebration of Oneness in
Marriage*. Colorado Springs, Colo.: Waterbrook Press, 2002.

2. Stanley, S. M., Markman, H. J., and Whitton, S. "Communication,
Conflict, and Commitment: Insights on the Foundations of
Relationship Success from a National Survey." *Family Process*,
2002, *41*(4), 659–675; Waite, L. J., and Joyner, K. "Emotional
Satisfaction and Physical Pleasure in Sexual Unions: Time
Horizon, Sexual Investment, and Sexual Exclusivity." *Journal of
Marriage and Family*, 2001, *63*, 247–264.

3. I can highly recommend the tape with both talks on it (and I do
not make any money by making this recommendation!). These
were both very potent and well-received talks. They are item
number 752-006, available online at www.Playbacknow.com or by
phone at (800)241-7785.

4. Smalley, G., and Trent, J. *The Blessing*. New York: Pocket, 1990.

5. Stanley, S. M., Trathen, D., McCain, S., and Bryan, M. *A Lasting Promise*. San Francisco: Jossey-Bass, 1998.

6. Leon Kass writes beautifully about this concept in *The Beginning of Wisdom* (New York: Free Press, 2003). Kass is a biologist with a deep understanding of Judaism and the Scriptures, and he writes from a philosophical and theological perspective about the relational teachings of Genesis. Although I am of a different theological (and scientific) bent than he, I found his work fascinating and touching.

CHAPTER THREE

1. Stanley, S. M., and Markman, H. J. "Assessing Commitment in Personal Relationships." *Journal of Marriage and Family*, 1992, 54, 595–608.

2. Jenkins, N. H., Stanley, S. M., Bailey, W. C., and Markman, H. J. *You Paid How Much for That?! How to Win at Money Without Losing at Love*. San Francisco: Jossey-Bass, 2002, p. 40.

3. Lane, R. E. (ed.). *The Loss of Happiness in Market Economies*. New Haven, Conn.: Yale University Press, 2000.

4. Such findings as this are covered very clearly in Waite, L., and Gallagher, M. *The Case for Marriage*. New York: Doubleday, 2000.

5. Waite and Gallagher, *The Case for Marriage*.

CHAPTER FOUR

1. This poem can be found in its entirety in MacDonald, G. *Knowing the Heart of God*. Minneapolis, Minn.: Bethany House, 2000, pp. 246–253.

2. Stanley, S. M., and Markman, H. J. "Assessing Commitment in Personal Relationships." *Journal of Marriage and Family*, 1992, 54, 595–608.

3. Covey, S. R., Merrill, A. R., and Merrill, R. R. *First Things First: To Live, to Love, to Learn, to Leave a Legacy.* New York: Free Press, 1996.

CHAPTER FIVE

1. Stanley, S. M., and Markman, H. J. "Assessing Commitment in Personal Relationships." *Journal of Marriage and Family*, 1992, *54*, 595–608; Stanley, S. M., Markman, H. J., and Whitton, S. "Communication, Conflict, and Commitment: Insights on the Foundations of Relationship Success from a National Survey." *Family Process*, 2002, *41*(4), 659–675.

2. Cook, K. S., and Emerson, R. M. "Power, Equity and Commitment in Exchange Networks." *American Sociological Review*, 1978, *43*, 721–739; Leik, R. K., and Leik, S. A. "Transition to Interpersonal Commitment." In R. L. Hamblin and J. H. Kunkel (eds.), *Behavioral Theory in Sociology.* New Brunswick, N.J.: Transaction Books, 1977.

3. Stanley and Markman, "Assessing Commitment in Personal Relationships"; Stanley, Markman, and Whitton, "Communication, Conflict, and Commitment."

4. Allen, E. S., and others. "Intrapersonal, Interpersonal, and Contextual Factors in Engaging in and Responding to Extramarital Involvement." *Clinical Psychology: Science and Practice*, forthcoming.

5. Johnson, D. J., and Rusbult, C. E. "Resisting Temptation: Devaluation of Alternative Partners as a Means of Maintaining Commitment in Close Relationships." *Journal of Personality and Social Psychology*, 1989, *57*, 967–980.

6. For example, see Edin, K., and Kefalas, M. J. *Promises I Can Keep: Why Poor Women Put Motherhood Before Marriage.* Los Angeles: University of California Press, forthcoming.

7. These two books written with my coauthors have extensive exercises for evaluating expectations: Markman, H. J., and others. *12 Hours to a Great Marriage*. San Francisco: Jossey-Bass, 2004; Stanley, S. M., Trathen, D., McCain, S., and Bryan, M. *A Lasting Promise*. San Francisco: Jossey-Bass, 1998.

CHAPTER SIX

1. Jones, W., and Adams, J. *Handbook of Interpersonal Commitment and Relationship Stability*. New York: Plenum, 1999; Levinger, G. "Marital Cohesiveness and Dissolution: An Integrative Review." *Journal of Marriage and Family*, 1965, 27, 19–28; Rusbult, C. E., and Buunk, B. P. "Commitment Processes in Close Relationships: An Interdependence Analysis." *Journal of Social and Personal Relationships*, 1993, 10, 175–204.

2. For example, see works focusing on what happens when people have strong insecurities about attachment to others: Cassidy, J., and Shaver, P. R. (eds.). *Handbook of Attachment: Theory, Research, and Clinical Applications*. New York: Guilford Press, 1998.

3. This notion is based on the principle of least interest formulated by Willard Waller; see Waller, W., and Hill, R. *The Family: A Dynamic Interpretation*. New York: Dryden, 1951.

4. Markman, H. J., and others. *12 Hours to a Great Marriage*. San Francisco: Jossey-Bass, 2004; Stanley, S. M., Trathen, D., McCain, S., and Bryan, M. *A Lasting Promise*. San Francisco: Jossey-Bass, 1998.

5. Stanley, S. M., and Markman, H. J. "Assessing Commitment in Personal Relationships." *Journal of Marriage and Family*, 1992, 54, 595–608.

6. Van Lange, P.A.M., and others. "From Game Theory to Real Life: How Social Value Orientation Affects Willingness to Sacrifice in Ongoing Close Relationships." *Journal of Personality and Social*

Psychology, 1997, *73*, 1330–1344; Van Lange, P.A.M., and others. "Willingness to Sacrifice in Close Relationships." *Journal of Personality and Social Psychology*, 1997, *72*, 1373–1395.

7. Whitton, S. W., Stanley, S. M., and Markman, H. J. "Sacrifice in Romantic Relationships: An Exploration of Relevant Research and Theory." In A. L. Vangelisti, H. T. Reis, and M. A. Fitzpatrick (eds.), *Stability and Change in Relationships*. New York: Cambridge University Press, 2002.

8. Ellison, C. G., and Anderson, K. L. "Religious Involvement and Domestic Violence Among U.S. Couples." *Journal for the Scientific Study of Religion*, 2001, *40*(2), 269–286; Ellison, C. G., Bartkowski, J. P., and Anderson, K. L. "Are There Religious Variations in Domestic Violence?" *Journal of Family Issues*, 1999, *20*(1), 87–113.

9. Dostoevsky, F. *The Brothers Karamazov*. New York: Barnes and Noble, 1950.

CHAPTER SEVEN

1. Doherty, W. J., and others. *Why Marriage Matters: Twenty-One Conclusions from the Social Sciences*. A Report from Family Scholars. New York: Institute for American Values, 2002; Stanton, G. *Why Marriage Matters*. Colorado Springs, Colo.: Pinon Press, 1997; Waite, L., and Gallagher, M. *The Case for Marriage*. New York: Doubleday, 2000.

2. Cummings, E. M., and Davies, P. *Children and Marital Conflict*. New York: Guilford Press, 1994; Emery, R. "Interparental Conflict and the Children of Discord and Divorce." *Psychological Bulletin*, 1982, *92*, 310–330; Grych, J., and Fincham, F. "Marital Conflict and Children's Adjustment." *Psychological Bulletin*, 1990, *108*, 267–290.

3. For example, see the books I cowrote with several colleagues that include large sections on handling conflict constructively:

Markman, H. J., Stanley, S. M., and Blumberg, S. L. *Fighting* for *Your Marriage.* San Francisco: Jossey-Bass, 2001; Stanley, S. M., Trathen, D., McCain, S., and Bryan, M. *A Lasting Promise.* San Francisco: Jossey-Bass, 1998.

4. Fincham, F. D. "Divorce." In N. J. Salkind (ed.), *Child Development: Macmillan Psychology Reference Series.* Farmington Hills, Mich.: Macmillan, 2002; Hetherington, E. M., and Kelly, J. *For Better or for Worse: Divorce Reconsidered.* New York: Norton, 2002; McLanahan, S., and Sandefur, G. *Growing Up with a Single Parent: What Hurts, What Helps.* Cambridge, Mass.: Harvard University Press, 1996; Stanley, S. M., and Fincham, F. D. "The Effects of Divorce on Children." *Couples Research and Therapy Newsletter* (AABT-SIG), 2002, *8*(1), 7–10 (available at www.PREPinc.com).

5. Cherlin, A. J., and Furstenberg, F. F., Jr. "Step Families in the United States: A Reconsideration." *Annual Review of Sociology,* 1994, *20*, 359–381.

6. Hetherington, E. M. "An Overview of the Virginia Longitudinal Study of Divorce and Remarriage with a Focus on the Early Adolescent." *Journal of Family Psychology,* 1993, 7, 39–56.

7. In addition to all the other references noted in this chapter, also see the following: Glenn, N. D., and Kramer, K. "The Marriages and Divorces of the Children of Divorce." *Journal of Marriage and Family,* 1987, *44*, 335–347; Halford, W. K., Sanders, M. R., and Behrens, B. C. "Repeating the Errors of Our Parents? Family of Origin Spouse Violence and Observed Conflict Management in Engaged Couples." *Family Process,* 2000, *39*, 219–235; Lawton, L. E., and Bures, R. "Parental Divorce and the 'Switching' of Religious Identity." *Journal for the Scientific Study of Religion,* 2001, *40*, 99–111.

8. Hetherington and Kelly, *For Better or for Worse;* Wallerstein, J. S., Lewis, J. M., and Blakeslee, S. *The Unexpected Legacy of Divorce: A Twenty-Five-Year Landmark Study.* New York: Hyperion, 2000.

9. Amato, P. R. "Good Enough Marriages: Parental Discord, Divorce, and Children's Well-Being." *Virginia Journal of Social Policy and the Law,* 2001, *9,* 71–94; also see Amato, P. R., and Booth, A. *A Generation at Risk: Growing Up in an Era of Family Upheaval.* Cambridge, Mass.: Harvard University Press, 1997.

10. A report based on this work is available at http://www.OKmarriage.org. For the major report from this work, please see Johnson, C. A., and Stanley, S. M. (eds.). *The Oklahoma Marriage Initiative Statewide Baseline Survey,* fall 2001.

11. Waite, L. J., and others. *Does Divorce Make People Happy? Findings from a Study of Unhappy Marriages.* New York: Institute for American Values, 2002.

12. Bach, R. *The Bridge Across Forever.* New York: Morrow, 1984.

13. Research suggests that people who are insecure about attachment are more prone to making errors in their relationships. Essentially, their neediness is so great that it clouds otherwise good judgment, such as about whom to marry in the first place. There are many research articles and scholarly works that show how important attachment—and attachment insecurity—can be in the decisions people make in their relationships. For example, Cassidy, J., and Shaver, P. R. *Handbook of Attachment Theory, Research, and Clinical Applications.* New York: Guilford Press, 1998; Davila, J., and Bradbury, T. N. "Attachment Insecurity and the Distinction Between Unhappy Spouses Who Do and Do Not Divorce." *Journal of Family Psychology,* 2001, *15,* 371–393; Johnson, S. M. *The Practice of Emotionally Focused Marital Therapy: Creating Connection.* New York: Taylor and Francis, 1996.

14. Love, P. *The Truth About Love*. New York: Fireside, 2001.

15. Johnson and others, *Marriage in Oklahoma*; see also http://marriage.rutgers.edu for a lot of great information on cohabitation and trends in marriage, divorce, and childbearing.

16. These findings are from many sources. The following are simply a sampling: Cohan, C., and Kleinbaum, S. "Toward a Greater Understanding of the Cohabitation Effect: Premarital Cohabitation and Marital Communication." *Journal of Marriage and Family*, 2002, *64*, 180–192; DeMaris, A., and Rao, V. "Premarital Cohabitation and Subsequent Marital Stability in the United States: A Reassessment." *Journal of Marriage and Family*, 1992, *54*(1), 178–190; Kline, G. H., and others. "Timing Is Everything: Pre-Engagement Cohabitation and Increased Risk for Poor Marital Outcomes." *Journal of Family Psychology*, 2004, *18*(2), 311–318; Forste, R., and Tanfer, K. "Sexual Exclusivity Among Dating, Cohabiting, and Married Women." *Journal of Marriage and Family*, 1996, *58*, 33–47; Stanley, S. M., Whitton, S. W., and Markman, H. J. "Maybe I Do: Interpersonal Commitment and Premarital or Nonmarital Cohabitation." *Journal of Family Issues*, 2004, *25*(4), 496–519; Thomson, E., and Colella, U. "Cohabitation and Marital Stability: Quality or Commitment?" *Journal of Marriage and Family*, 1992, *54*(2), 259–267.

17. Kline and others, "Timing Is Everything."

18. Stanley, Whitton, and Markman, "Maybe I Do."

19. Johnson and others, *Marriage in Oklahoma*.

20. Axinn, W. G., and Barber, J. S. "Living Arrangements and Family Formation Attitudes in Early Adulthood." *Journal of Marriage and Family*, 1997, *59*(3), 595–611.

21. Lillard, L. A., Brien, M. J., and Waite, L. J. "Premarital Cohabitation and Subsequent Marital Dissolution: A Matter of

Self-Selection?" *Demography*, 1995, *32*(3), 437–457; Stanley, Whitton, and Markman, "Maybe I Do."

22. For example, Cohan and Kleinbaum, "Toward a Greater Understanding of the Cohabitation Effect."

23. Stanley, S. M., and Markman, H. J. *Marriage in the 90s: A Nationwide Random Phone Survey.* Denver, Colo.: PREP, 1997.

24. Manning, W. D., and Smock, P. J. "Measuring and Modeling Cohabitation: New Perspectives from Qualitative Data." Paper presented at the Healthy Marriage Interventions and Evaluation symposium of the Measurement Issues in Family Demography Conference, Washington, D.C., Nov. 2003.

25. One of the most important findings of ongoing research by Pamela Smock and Wendy Manning is that many people say that their cohabiting did not involve a clear decision—much less one based on a strong commitment—but that it merely happened; see Manning, W. D., and Smock, P. J. "Measuring and Modeling Cohabitation: New Perspectives from Qualitative Data." Paper presented at the Healthy Marriage Interventions and Evaluation symposium of the Measurement Issues in Family Demography conference, Washington, D.C., Nov. 2003.

26. One person who has gotten a lot of positive attention for examining the topic of how to choose a mate and providing ideas for people is John Van Epp. You can find out more about his model for avoiding someone who will not be good for you at http://www.nojerks.com. Many of my colleagues really appreciate his material, in which the level of commitment in a relationship figures prominently.

27. *A Lasting Promise, Fighting* for *Your Marriage*, and *12 Hours to a Great Marriage*, published by Jossey-Bass, all contain this detailed exercise.

CHAPTER EIGHT

1. Seldes, G. *The Great Thoughts.* New York: Ballantine, 1985, pp. 185–186.

2. Sir Winston Churchill, quoted in *Reader's Digest*, Dec. 1954.

3. Sir Winston Churchill, first wartime address, Guildhall, London, Sept. 4, 1914, from *Columbia World of Quotations*, at http://www.bartleby.com/66/67/12367.html.

4. Sir Winston Churchill, speech to the House of Commons, June 18, 1940, from *Columbia World of Quotations*, at http://www.bartleby.com/66/62/12362.html.

5. For a discussion of the different kinds of divorce rates, see this document on our website: "What Really Is the Divorce Rate?" at www.prepinc.com/main/Articles.asp.

6. See U. S. Census data as of the mid-1990s, reported in http://www.census.gov/population/www/documentation/twps0020 /twps0020.html#abstract.

7. Whitehead and Popenoe of the National Marriage Project have compiled various citations related to this trend and provide the data in a very accessible manner. They chart the trends in Whitehead, B. D., and Popenoe, D. *The State of Our Unions: The Social Health of Marriage in America* (with *Essay: Marriage and Children: Coming Together Again?*). Piscataway, N.J.: National Marriage Project, 2002; available at http://marriage.rutgers.edu.

8. Whitehead and Popenoe, *The State of Our Unions.*

9. Whitehead and Popenoe, *The State of Our Unions.*

10. The evidence for the benefits of marriage are laid out very well in two books that are written for the nontechnical reader. I can highly recommend both: Stanton, G. *Why Marriage Matters.* Colorado Springs, Colo.: Pinon Press, 1997; Waite, L., and Gallagher, M. *The Case for Marriage.* New York: Doubleday, 2000.

11. Sir Winston Churchill, *Time*, Sept. 12, 1960.

12. Stanley, S. M., Whitton, S. W., and Markman, H. J. "Maybe I Do: Interpersonal Commitment and Premarital or Nonmarital Cohabitation." *Journal of Family Issues*, 2004, *25*, 496–519.

13. Stanley, S. M., Lobitz, W. C., and Dickson, F. "Using What We Know: Commitment and Cognitions in Marital Therapy." In W. Jones and J. Adams (eds.), *Handbook of Interpersonal Commitment and Relationship Stability*. New York: Plenum, 1999.

14. Call, V. R., and Heaton, T. B. "Religious Influence on Marital Stability." *Journal for the Scientific Study of Religion*, 1997, *36*, 382–392; Clements, M. L., Stanley, S. M., and Markman, H. J. "Before They Said 'I Do': Discriminating Among Marital Outcomes over Thirteen Years Based on Premarital Data." *Journal of Marriage and Family*, 2004, *66*, 613–626; Hunt, R. A., and King, M. B. "Religiosity and Marriage." *Journal for the Scientific Study of Religion*, 1978, *17*, 399–406; Lehrer, E. L., and Chiswick, C. "Religion as a Determinant of Marital Stability." *Demography*, 1993, *30*, 385–404.

15. See, for example, Heaton, T. B., and Pratt, E. L. "The Effects of Religious Homogamy on Marital Satisfaction and Stability." *Journal of Family Issues*, 1990, *11*, 191–207.

16. Mahoney, A., and others. "Marriage and the Spiritual Realm: The Role of Proximal and Distal Religious Constructs in Marital Functioning." *Journal of Family Psychology*, 1999, *13*(3), 321–338.

CHAPTER NINE

1. For example, Fincham, F. D. "The Kiss of the Porcupines: From Attributing Responsibility to Forgiving." *Personal Relationships*, 2000, 7, 1–23; McCullough, M. E., Worthington, E. L., Jr., and Rachal, K. C. "Interpersonal Forgiving in Close Relationships." *Journal of Personality and Social Psychology*, 1997, *73*, 321–336.

CHAPTER TEN

1. I got the idea for the term *relationship capital* after reading a discussion of social capital in Barbara Dafoe Whitehead's book *The Divorce Culture* (New York: Knopf, 1997).

2. Jenkins, N. H., Stanley, S. M., Bailey, W. C., and Markman, H. J. *You Paid How Much for That?! How to Win at Money Without Losing at Love.* San Francisco: Jossey-Bass, 2002; Stanton, G. *Why Marriage Matters.* Colorado Springs, Colo.: Pinon Press, 1997; Waite, L., and Gallagher, M. *The Case for Marriage.* New York: Doubleday, 2000.

3. Godsey, D. "Winning Strategies for the Next Ten Years in the Financial World: 'Long Term' Can Mean Six Months from Now." *Fortune*, Dec. 12, 1995, p. 66.

4. Gottman, J. "Lessons from the Love Lab." Plenary address to the Smart Marriages, Happy Families conference, Washington, D.C., May 1997.

5. Jordan, P., Stanley, S. M., and Markman, H. J. *Becoming Parents.* San Francisco: Jossey-Bass, 1999; Cowan, C. P., and Cowan, P. A. *When Partners Become Parents: The Big Life Change for Couples.* New York: HarperCollins, 1992.

6. Markman, H. J., and others. *12 Hours to a Great Marriage.* San Francisco: Jossey-Bass, 2004; Stanley, S. M., Trathen, D., McCain, S., and Bryan, M. *A Lasting Promise.* San Francisco: Jossey-Bass, 1998.

7. One scholar who has been emphasizing rituals a great deal lately is Bill Doherty. One of his excellent books is *Take Back Your Marriage.* New York: Guilford Press, 2003.

8. I was first exposed to this idea by my colleague Howard Markman. He and Cliff Notarius have taught for years that Tolstoy was wrong when he said, in the opening of *Anna Karenina*, that "All happy families resemble one another, but each unhappy family is

unhappy in its own way." Not true, Markman and Notarius argue. It is just the opposite. Couples who are destroying their marriages over time look pretty much like other couples who have done the same. You see either growing distance or increasing conflict—or both. There is nothing very mysterious or magical about this. Yet couples who have wonderful, thriving marriages all look different. The diversity of marriages is a positive feature, where each couple has the chance to develop their own unique blend of elements to make a work of beauty. But this blending happens only when partners feel the deep sense of security in their future together that allows each to be accepted by the other and to give this acceptance in return. See Notarius, C., and Markman, H. J. *We Can Work It Out: Making Sense of Marital Conflict.* New York: Putnam, 1993.

CHAPTER ELEVEN

1. Johnson, C. A., and Stanley, S. M. (eds.). *The Oklahoma Marriage Initiative Statewide Baseline Survey*, fall 2001 (available at http://www.OKmarriage.org).

2. Markman, H. J., and others. *12 Hours to a Great Marriage.* San Francisco: Jossey-Bass, 2004; Stanley, S. M., Trathen, D., McCain, S., and Bryan, M. *A Lasting Promise.* San Francisco: Jossey-Bass, 1998.

3. A sermon by a pastor named Alex Strauch led me to see the beauty and simplicity of this passage and how the map I discuss in this chapter could be applied to marriage.

• RESOURCES •

My colleagues and I have many additional resources available; I have included the following section so you can go further if you wish, either as an individual or couple interested in learning more about how to make a great marriage, or as one who helps couples strengthen their relationships.

In addition to the book you are holding, there are many other titles that are part of our overall effort to put research-based ideas and strategies into the hands of couples. You can find out more about these books by calling our company, PREP, at 800-366-0166, by calling Jossey-Bass at 415-433-1740, by going online to www.PREPinc.com, or by contacting any bookstore.

12 Hours to a Great Marriage, by H. J. Markman, S. M. Stanley, S. L. Blumberg, N. H. Jenkins, and C. Whiteley, is a comprehensive set of strategies for those who want to build their marriages through learning how to manage the problems of life well and also by learning how to preserve and protect all the great stuff of marriage—the fun, friendship, and commitment.

Fighting for *Your Marriage*, by H. J. Markman, S. M. Stanley, and S. L. Blumberg, is the original, flagship book in our series of books designed to help couples lower their odds of marital distress and problems and thrive in living life well, together. It has been recently updated and is a classic in our field.

A Lasting Promise: A Christian Guide to Fighting for *Your Marriage*, by S. M. Stanley, D. Trathen, S. McCain, and

M. Bryan, is founded on a Christian theological perspective of marriage, and fully integrates that with sound marital research and the strategies of the PREP approach.

Becoming Parents: How to Strengthen Your Marriage as Your Family Grows, by P. L. Jordan, S. M. Stanley, and H. J. Markman, is the same approach adapted for couples as they become parents.

You Paid How *Much for That?! How to Win at Money Without Losing at Love*, by N. H. Jenkins, S. M. Stanley, W. C. Bailey, and H. J. Markman, teaches couples how to conquer money issues using the PREP approach. (This book is now available only through our website or 800 number.)

PREP
P.O. Box 102530
Denver, CO 80250-2530
E-mail: info@PREPinc.com
Website: www.PREPinc.com
800-366-0166

• ABOUT SCOTT M. STANLEY
AND GARY SMALLEY •

Scott M. Stanley, Ph.D., is codirector of the Center for Marital and Family Studies at the University of Denver. He has published widely, including research journals, book chapters, and works for couples, with a focus on commitment theory, communication, conflict, and sacrifice. Stanley has worked extensively with the various branches of the U.S. armed forces in helping young military couples build and protect their marriages. He is also a senior program adviser to the Oklahoma Marriage Initiative, which is unfolding one of the most comprehensive and strategic marriage initiatives ever attempted.

Along with Dr. Howard Markman and colleagues, Stanley has been involved in the research, development, and refinement of the Prevention and Relationship Enhancement Program (PREP) since 1977. PREP is an internationally known program aimed at preventing marital distress and is the basis for the best-selling book *Fighting for Your Marriage*. Stanley is the coauthor of that book and several others for couples, including *A Lasting Promise*, *Becoming Parents*, and *12 Hours to a Great Marriage*, all published by Jossey-Bass. He has regularly appeared in both print and broadcast media as an expert on marriage, including in the *New York Times*, *USA Today*, the *Washington Times*, the *Wall Street Journal*, *Psychology Today*, *Redbook*, *Ladies Home Journal*, and *Marriage Partnership*.

Gary Smalley is one of the best-known authors and speakers on marriage and loving relationships in the world today. He has authored or coauthored over thirty-five best-selling books, along with many popular films and videos. He has spent over forty years learning, teaching, and counseling. Smalley has personally interviewed hundreds of singles and couples and has surveyed thousands of people at his seminars, asking two questions: What strengthens your relationships? What weakens them? From his wealth of experience, he has found powerful ways to convey to couples all over the world the principles and values that sustain intimacy and commitment in marriage.

Smalley has developed a new, powerful, live two-day seminar based on his recent book, *The DNA of Relationships*. The book is based on six life-changing principles that can dissuade a couple from divorce in just four days. The same six principles are changing singles as young as ten years of age to mature loving individuals.

His award-winning video series, *Hidden Keys to Loving Relationships*, has been seen by millions of couples who have benefited from Smalley's wisdom and humor to help them build their marriages and key relationships. Smalley has appeared on national television programs such as *Oprah*, *Larry King Live*, *Extra*, *Today Show*, and *Sally Jessy Raphael*, as well as numerous national radio programs. He has been featured on hundreds of regional and local television and radio programs across the United States. Smalley and his wife, Norma, have been married for forty years and live in Branson, Missouri. They have three grown children—Kari, Greg, and Michael—who participate full-time in Smalley's marriage and family work. Most important, they have eight grandchildren.